What Others Are Saying
About Rowena Starling and This Book

"Rowena totally rocked our event. She makes real connections with the audience and gives them tangible tools they can use right away."

~ Jessica Hadari, Founder of FemTalks

"Rowena really helped me through dealing with the problems one of my daughters was having. She helped me through that, and *everything* in my life is better because of her help, including parenting. I highly recommend her as a guide for any parent."

~ Louise Edington, Parent and Life Path Catalyst at Your Cosmic Blueprint

"I'd like to write a belated testimonial for Rowena Starling's amazing work. I spent about a half hour on the phone with her and picked my deepest fear to work on. During the process Rowena took me through, I went from, 'Whoa! I can barely stand to think about this!' to 'What were we talking about? Oh, that old thing…!' Incredible beyond words. If I had a thousand tongues to say thank you with, it wouldn't be enough. All I can say is don't miss this magical opportunity to have instant change in your life."

~ Joanne Butcher, Filmmaker Success Coach at Filmmaker Success: Creating Films that Change the World and Make Money

"Rowena is true to who she is. I can always count on that. I love her acts of kindness. They encourage me when words won't do."

~ Sandra Lane, Library Specialist

"After my call yesterday with the lovely Rowena Starling, I landed a big step forward for me—old Sarah had an irrational fear of speaking about vulnerability and being seen. I felt the fear melt out of my body after just thirty minutes of (intense) fear-release work with Rowena. Which worked wonders! I feel things have improved. I have been doing more out of my shell like participating in a song ceremony I previously would have shied away from. It has been interesting. I feel the fear has been released and I am adjusting to a new way of being."

~ Sarah Montano, Bozeman, Montana

"My fear of dating is *gone*! Thanks for asking. I'm dating a great guy at the moment and having a lot of fun!"

~ Denise Carbon, Founder, Developmental Specialist, Life and Parent Coach at Special Advantage with Denise Carbon

"I can say that I really don't feel any more fear of running out of money since our session. In fact, I am more relaxed and at ease about it than I've been for a long time—and not because I've come into sudden wealth. What I have found is I have been taking actions to untangle myself from excessive financial commitments and am now living within my means—which I was not when Rowena gave me my session. I have gotten clearer about what I need for my foundation, and actually more committed to providing that for myself. I have received a job offer as a result of prioritizing and looking for a better, non-commissioned based job—a job that feels grounded. Thank you, Rowena, for that fast shift. It seems to have really worked!"

~ Justine Renson, San Francisco, California

"It really helped! Such a gift, shifting my fear around asking for my value and getting compensation for it. Thank you!"

~ Quinn Morgan, Principal at Quinn Morgan Designs

"Rowena Starling has saved my life! I overcame my underwater fear (one year and four months ahead of my goal). Just swam laps at the community pool this morning! Thank you for helping me realize something on my vision board. Thanks for gettin' a girl to swim again!"

~ Dr. Claudine Buglisi

"Rowena's personality and her ability to get along with people and work with anyone and everyone are her greatest gifts. And she's determined and patient."

~ David Broady, Oakland, California

"One of Rowena's strengths is she is continually seeking ways to better herself spiritually. Her talents are many, but the one that strikes me the most is her ability to laugh so deeply at all of life's experiences. Her other abilities are as parent, artist, healer, and financial expert, to name a few."

~ *Craig Brandt, Attorney-at-Law*

"My incredible, gifted Aries woman friend has unshakable vision and resolve to see that vision manifested. Her ideas are truly unique and things the world truly *does* need. She is bull-doggedly tenacious. Anything she puts her mind to will happen. I am constantly surprised and inspired by this particular gift of hers and wish I could emulate it. She never quits. She gives fully each and every time, showing incredible trust and vulnerability without fear. She expects others to do the same without excuses. She is creative, finding the resources to do what needs to be done. And in not-so-shabby fashion, it's always quality. She is loving, cares deeply, and is white-hot in her thoughts, expressions, and ideas. She builds and shares her bridges. All the people close to her benefit from her harvests."

~ *Kymi Armour, Digital Creator & Songstress at KymiArmour.com*

"Rowena is generous, color-blind, and persistent. She doesn't whine, complain, or blame others for what's going on in her life. She has a good sense of humor and is as happy to laugh at other people's jokes as at her own. She listens. I experience her as optimistic while at the same time realistic—a good combo, I think."

~ Karin Ireland, IrelandCommunications.com

"I believe any of my descriptions of Rowena could go under more than one heading: her strengths—people person, confident, equitable, honest; her talents—creative, creates a win-win situation, direct, no bullshit, believes in what she's doing, her abilities—completes the task at hand, tries to make each situation equitable."

~ James Becker, Palm Springs, California

"I perceive Rowena to be a deep person at all times. She has a talent for digging deep into the mind and soul and bringing out thoughts in people that they didn't even know existed. This talent allows her to meet no strangers. Her interaction with people of all ages, cultures, races, and creeds is proof. Her ability to lead and take charge reveals her strong and domineering attitude that shows her strength in rectifying any situation, good or bad, and the ability to hang in there throughout the duration. Her artistic talents are amazing and are shown through her paintings, cooking, free-for-all lifestyle, and attitude on life in general."

~ Norma Starling, Tech Specialist

"In *Being a Parent Sucks...Sometimes,* Rowena Starling reveals that parenting can be a lot more fulfilling when we realize it is a calling to raise God's children. Full of effective techniques to regain your peace of mind, get your children to listen to you, and to reduce your stress, this book will benefit you whether you have one newborn child or a half-dozen adult children."

~ *Patrick Snow, Publishing Coach and International Best-Selling Author of* Creating Your Own Destiny *and* The Affluent Entrepreneur

"Rowena Starling writes honestly about her own parenting ups and downs as well as those of other parents she has known and helped. From humorous stories of what went wrong to truths sometimes hard to accept, such as that trying to be our child's friend is a mistake, she reveals a path to parenthood that will bring you peace of mind and a calm center to do better from."

~ *Nicole Gabriel, Author of* Finding Your Inner Truth *and* Stepping Into Your Becoming

"In this book, Rowena Starling warns us not to buy into the myths that parenting has to be hard. She offers sage advice on how to break the cycle of generational trauma with your own children, how to teach your children to meditate and be in touch with their intuition, and even how to get a better handle on your finances so you can focus on quality time with your children rather than worrying. Being a parent doesn't have to suck; it can be a lot easier when you follow the advice in these pages."

~ *Tyler R. Tichelaar, PhD and Award-Winning Author of* Narrow Lives *and* The Best Place

BEING A PARENT SUCKS ...SOMETIMES

18
TIPS TO TRANSFORM YOUR PAIN TO PEACE

ROWENA STARLING

AVIVA PUBLISHING
New York

BEING A PARENT SUCKS…Sometimes
18 Tips to Transform Your Pain to Peace

Published by:
Aviva Publishing
Lake Placid, NY
(518) 523-1320
www.AvivaPubs.com

Rowena Starling
(510) 779-2486
Rowena@RowenaStarling.com
www.BeingaParentSucksSometimes.com
www.RowenaStarling.com

ISBN: 978-1-63618-307-7
Library of Congress: 2023921504
Editor: Superior Book Productions

Cover Designer: Nicole Gabriel, Angel Dog Productions
Interior Book Layout: Nicole Gabriel, Angel Dog Productions
Author Photo: Janet Becker

Every attempt has been made to properly source all quotes.
Printed in the United States of America
First Edition
2 4 6 8 10

DEDICATION

To My Dear Mother:
You are long gone, but I must *thank you* publicly for bringing my life forward. I know you can "hear" me. I finally understand.

To Mother Surratt:
The type of mother I wish my mother had known.

To You, The Reader:
May this book be a resource to help you become an even better parent.

ACKNOWLEDGMENTS

To my dear friend Stuart Reinsch: Thank you for being so supportive of me in my many endeavors over the years! I appreciate your patience and enlightened example. You have a beautiful heart that shows us all how to radiate steadfast friendship to everyone who would receive it.

To Barbara and Alonzo Fields: I thank you, my loving friends, who kept me from complete homelessness.

I'd also like to thank: Byron and Norma Starling, Yolonda Richmond, Jesus Christ, Mr. Angle, Ms. Rice, Ms. Scranton, Ms. Bailey, Ms. Robey, Bernie and September Dohrman, Neville Goddard, Shunryu Suzuki, Jill Lublin, Randy Peyser, Christine Bronstein, Marta Maria Marraccini, Tiffany Largie, Adryenn Ashley, Avis Oglesby, Les Brown, Judy Feldenhausen, Maharishi Mahesh Yogi, Jiddu Krishnamurti, Dr. Deepak Chopra, Brenda Surratt, Judy Cohen, Howard Surratt, Sr., Shakti Gawain, Sadhguru, Mary Sackett, Rumi, Anita Rowell, James Dygert, Jackie Lapin, Gerry Foster, Hugh Ballou, Harry Lay, Mark and Erica Dedon, T. Harv Eker, Valencia Ray, Lindsay Albert, Dr. Joe Vitale, Dr. Philip McGraw, Tonya Dawn Recla, Mother Teresa, Oprah Winfrey, Catherine Varnau, Og Mandino, Donna Pierson, Bob Procter, Michael and Katherine Miller, Reverend Cristhal Bennett, Rachelle Lee, Anne Reinsch, Craig Brandt, Mark Sackett, Patsy and Dewit Attwood, Debra Caywood Rukas, Shemone Buie-Valdes, Sigrid Reinsch, Linda Ann Banks, Reverend Steven and Stephanie Willis, Martin Altherr, Jim Rohn, Maria Speth, Carol Bell, Greg Sorensen, Maurice Smallwood,

Regina Wollenberg, Joie Seldon, Ju D Young, Louise Hay, Leila Radan, Dr. Lynette Francis, Virginia Butler, John C. Maxwell, Kweli Gibson, Roynita Daniels, Michael Tummings, Steve Harvey, Molly and Kevin Maguire, W. Clement Stone, Peter Reinsch, Sandra and Michael Lane, Patty and Henry Kates, Penny Anderson, Lynette Watson, ShaSha Watson, Sharon Tom, Sophia van Leeuwen, Teresa Marchese, Jay Mercado, Frank and Ella Porep, Reverend Linda Gruel, Wil Ash, Brian Tracy, and Zig Ziglar.

Thank you also to:

Patrick Snow for his patient guidance through the writing/publishing process.

Tyler Tichelaar and Larry Alexander for their amazing editing skills. Without their talent, this book would just be an incomplete Word document on my laptop.

Nicole Gabriel for her beautiful cover and the interior design of this book.

CONTENTS

Introduction

SEEING YOUR PARENT EXPERIENCE

"If a child enters your life,
it is time to relearn the life you have forgotten."

~ Sadhguru

Which of these three situations best describes you?

1.) You are parenting by default. You're winging it as a parent (or did if your child is an adult) and are out of your mind with stress. You are fully aware you don't know what you're doing, and you're grasping at straws and searching all over the internet for answers. You feel like a failure.

2.) You think you've got a handle on it, but it's all too much and, quite frankly, *the kids are running you.* You feel a little helpless, a little sleep-deprived, and a lot broke.

3.) You're the parent of an adult wondering what happened to the peace of mind part that was supposed to happen once the kids reached adulthood. You may be an empty-nester or your adult kids and/or their kids still live with you. Perhaps your parents are there or need your care as well.

What do you want? Is it money? A mate? Family? Fame? Peace of mind? All of these and more? What do you *want*? Before you read farther, make a list of the family-related things you want.

What are you asking for, praying for? What do you want for your life and your offspring's lives? (I use the word "offspring" to include adult children.) Look, I've been there. I did most of all three of the above.

GREAT UNIVERSAL QUESTIONS

The great universal questions you may be asking yourself are:

- "What's in this parent game for me?"
- "Why should I bend myself out of shape to accommodate this process?"
- "Don't I have enough to do?"

What's in this parent game for you is a "yes" to your ultimate happiness and life fulfillment. It's a "yes" to the reason (happiness) you should bend yourself out of shape to accommodate this process. "Why" is "yes" to the continuation of your family line and your contribution to the expansion of the human race. Yes, you have enough to do and more to do, and even if you have no child, you'd still have "enough" to do, so why not do this bit of God's bidding?

Doing the best you can at being a parent improves your life and all of the lives around you. In this book, you will learn how to have peace as a parent and as a person. You will learn how to shed/eliminate the fears that are blocking your joy and peace. You will learn how to get what you want and parent at the same time, solve your issues with your child listening to you, get a handle on discipline, and teach your child respect. Oh! And finances—you need to raise the child and the dough. You will learn how to put a system in place so that a lot of chaos is avoided and, as time passes, running the household gets easier. You will learn how to make your life easier in general.

There's a ripple effect...a paying it forward that helps to secure your future. Our children are our future. They will support us then as we support our parents and grandparents now; for some this support is quite literal, and I am not speaking necessarily about finances. Your greater mission is the expansion of human intelligence and experience. That is done through the birth of humans, generation after generation.

What's in being a parent for you? It's the revisiting of nourishing moments you forget to appreciate, moment to moment, day in and day out. Nourishing moments…like the feeling of the waves of unconditional love that wash through you when your baby smiles at you for the first time, the forced patience that makes you sit quietly and calm down, or the realization that someone else is right and no one has to be wrong. Unconditional love feeds your soul and your cells. Deliberately remembering and inducing this feeling helps you maintain your health and happiness. It's the nourishment of your spirit, the expansion of your soul, the joy that brings prosperity, and the essence of peace, which is the peace beyond all understanding that induces a quiet mind and calm feelings. It's when you let go and let God handle your life a lot more. As you read these pages, you will be helped in integrating the ease that is natural to being a parent and a human.

This book is an edited collection of various articles I've written over the last ten years about transforming your pain into peace by getting to the center of relaxation and ease. *The names of people have been changed to protect the innocent.* I am sharing what I have experienced, researched, and observed over seventy-three-plus years (more than half of those years have been as a mother) to help you release your pain and fears and gain, naturally, the peace that is readily available and that you so richly deserve. Like you, I had regrets over my imperfections as a parent. The twenty-twenty hindsight offered in this book can help current nurturing parents eliminate and avoid unnecessary pain and parents of adults get over their perceived mistakes that are causing pain and avoidable chronic disease today.

I don't have all the answers. I'm still learning and open to learning from you. Your situation is unique to you. There's a world of answers to specific problems provided out there. You're busy. The information in this book endeavors to help you narrow your searches and save yourself some time.

Make a point of doing the exercises at the end of each chapter to deepen your "shedding" process. I'm available to coach you through it if you need. Are you ready to begin? Let's go!

Ultimately, there is only one thing to understand, as you will discover in these pages.

Chapter 1

HAVING PEACE AS A PARENT

"God doesn't call the qualified. He qualifies the called."

~ Reverend Michael Beckwith

BEING A PARENT IS A CALLING

You were born to be a hero to your child. Reverend Michael Beckwith said, "God doesn't call the qualified. He qualifies the called." I believe this is true. Not all people are called to be parents. Many parents don't pick up the mantle of being *responsible parents*, heroes for their children, and our world suffers because of it. Of the ones called, a heroic task is laid before them…to bring up the next generation of heroes.

A clear result I want you to achieve from this book is the minimization of stress through the recognition that being a parent is a "calling." It is a strong urge toward a particular way of life, which is the very definition of a "calling." It's "a way of life" because once a parent, always a parent. It is a call from the "Deep Joyous Subconscious Core" of ourselves, also known as Source, God, Allah, etc. that is insistent on producing more of our species on this planet. That is where the strong urge comes from (via hormones). Chuck life as you once knew it. It's over.

What do you think being a parent is all about?

In 1990, as I sat on the back deck drowning in worry and feeling overwhelmed over how I would make ends meet, my six-year-old son bounced out of the back door wanting something—I don't remember what, but probably attention. I sent him on his merry way with a "yes" to whatever it was he asked for and wondered, *Why isn't this parenting thing on the six o'clock news every night?*

The sheer weight of the responsibility of taking care of my son haunted me every waking moment, and it often caused me to be distracted and impatient with him. I was *not* at peace as a parent. I recognized my son needed more loving attention from me, but I didn't have a handle on what it would take to give it to him. I needed more than anything to be at peace with my financial circumstances. The money problem was making all kinds of noise in my head, heart, and feelings!

One of the most powerful ways parental peace is realized is when you understand that being a parent is a calling. When you can relax into your parent mindset, you receive and enjoy peace in a deep and abiding way.

"I know you're tired but come.
This is the way."
~ Rumi

As a parent, you are, after all, heavily influencing God's Blessed Progeny (as you are God's Blessed Progeny yourself). Your Deep Joyous Subconscious Core is thoroughly connected to Our Source, God, Pure Consciousness, The Universe, Allah—however you address where everything comes from. No way are you dangling out here rudderless. You've just forgotten whom you're attached to! When being a parent is viewed and felt this way, the experience takes on a sacredness because you understand and appreciate you are not working at this alone.

THE ULTIMATE POWER...

The Ultimate Power is part of your core and can be accessed with your feelings to make your experience easier, if you allow it. It's up to you to recognize it and give yourself permission to take a break when you need and/or want one. Relax.... Breathe....

"The more knowledge you have that your conscious and subconscious mind can access and make sense of, the more knowledge you have the potential of decoding and accessing from the superconscious."

~ Adam Higson

What Adam Higson means in the quote above is your relaxing, breathing, and going within make it easier to access all of the information and help you need from Source. My emotional pain forced me to go within. I had no choice. I was grasping at straws outside of me!

Case in point: A couple felt guilty over the way they had parented their two sons. Once the sons became adults, one of the sons never spoke to them, and the other was a raging alcoholic. This caused them tremendous grief and loneliness and serious health issues. When they got in touch with their Deep Joyous Subconscious Core and hung out there most of the time, their hearts were eased and their relationships with their sons softened.

They hung out in Silence, not just in their twenty-minute meditations, but also as they went about the activities of their day. As they started to receive what they wanted with their sons, their health improved, and their daily practice took on a feeling of being sacred and special. That sacredness dictates peace to your whole experience and helps you minimize stress. (By the way, not all stress is toxic and poisonous. There is good stress. It's called eustress and is basically the low-level stress that causes us to get stuff done. It's stress, also known as motivation, that we like.)

WHAT IS SACRED?

"I've learned that people will forget what you said,
people will forget what you did,
but people will never forget how you made them feel."

~ Maya Angelou

The quote above is true for your offspring as well, even more so because your voice echoes in your children's heads even into adulthood. What are you saying to them? They may or may not forget what you did, but they will never forget how you made them feel, ever. Think of your own parents....

What is written on your heart and soul that you want to see bloom in the heart and soul of your family, your offspring?

Many parents think the idea of peace in being a parent is an oxymoron, a contradiction, but really, it's a divine exercise in recognizing the power you carry deep within your joyous core self, nourishing that in yourself, and then transferring that nourishing recognition to your offspring. If you just tap into that power and let go of feeling the need to control everything, you will have more peace and freedom.

Look, I understand. I've been there. I was once buried in emotional turmoil and financial ruin from divorcing my son's father. My worry and anxiety about being able to properly care for and protect my baby were overwhelming! He was only three at the time. He's more than thirty now and a happy independent adult.

For more than half of our children, high levels of stress are being passed on from the parents! More than half of us parents are stressed at unhealthy levels! How many reports have we heard of parents accidentally leaving their child in the car in the heat all day as they work in the office or shop in the mall? How many children are deliberately killed by their stressed parents? More than 500 per year! It behooves us to get a firm handle on this stress problem for their sake as well as for ours.

ARE YOU TIRED?

Exhausted? Are you sitting there stressed out of your gourd asking, "How am I supposed to do anything with kids crawling all over me?" or "How can I possibly get over what my teen (or adult child) is doing?"

Know you are not working this deal alone. Relax and know that. Let the kids crawl all over you; stop what you're doing and enjoy it! (Even if you're reading this book.) They won't be that size for very long. If they're in their teens, relax and remember yourself at that age. Act wisely. If they're adults, let go and let God.

Know that your progress is not stopped or even slowed by *your loving interaction* with your offspring. When you maintain a quiet mind, progress and success are happening regardless of what you do, especially when you're feeling relaxed.

What slows your progress toward your goals is not knowing and understanding your true divine nature. Here's my experience with this....

Many times, even after learning and understanding meditation and my connection to the Divine, I would make tremendous progress to the point of miracles and then slip back into forgetting. When I am centered in the peaceful feeling I get from my Deep, Joyous Subconscious Core, what I want happens easily and effortlessly. When I slip into forgetting that, progress slows down, and I go into struggle and effort.

Understand you are not working on this deal alone. The Ultimate Power, your Godhead, can be accessed with your feelings to make your experience easier if you allow it. It's up to you to recognize it and give yourself permission to take a break. Relax. Breathe.

Be okay with your teen or adult offspring venting or doing whatever they're doing while you get yourself together. When you change, everyone changes! It is the Law of Divine Influence, also known as the Law of Attraction. We're all connected.

DIVINE INFLUENCE

Divine influence gives you the ease you're looking for because if you're looking for ease, what you want will be attracted to you. What you want for yourself and your family then appears and gives you the juice to sprint forward with joy and glee. As you sprint, you take your child with you!

Stop your mind right now and get off the misery roller coaster. Your mind is not the boss of you. Let the power of your innate, positive, Deep Joyous Subconscious Core be the boss of you.

Stop your mind right now for thirty seconds....

What did you notice? What did you feel?

If your mind didn't stop, it means you must practice controlling it. Consistent meditation will help you gain control. Silencing your mind is the key to gaining peace, and it's where the magic is. Gaining peace promotes health, wealth, and a happy family.

Your assignment is to "be in quiet mind" all day unless you're in creating mode. This is your new practice. Creation, also known as work, often requires thought that is not quiet. This kind of noise is okay.

When you frame your parenting experience as a "calling," you can answer the call by getting out of the way a little bit and letting the *easy* winds of divine purpose blow through your activities. You can engage creativity in your parent role and inspire your children to curry your favor (which means they're more cooperative).

Do you think your children are oblivious to you? They are watching your every move! Let them be inspired by how you relate to them.

On the other side of fatigue is the breath of fresh air, the surge of energy, and more cooperation from your babies than you now see. As the old English proverb says, "Fear knocked at the door. Faith answered. There was no one there."

You can open the closet door to where the money boogey lives and find there is no one there. Punch through the thin coating of the "poor health" illusion and find your strong, robust self.

A single father was having a very trying time with his son, so he was shocked to learn from his son's teacher how his son was bragging to the other kids about what a hero his dad is. The father was shocked to hear this because prior to our time together, he and his twelve-year-old son were at loggerheads over the son's behavior issues and refusal to cooperate.

Once Dad started to engage, communicate, and listen more, he learned his son was being bullied. He gave his son some "dad pointers" on how to handle himself, and the bullying and tons of family stress rolled away. He became a superhero to his son for solving that problem. He had come to his son's rescue.

Do you know you are a hero? Imagine a world where *all* parents recognized our divine calling to raise the next generation of heroes. Can you see world peace in our grasp if we seize the opportunity to make being a parent be easier, leading to more loving family relationships overall? Your part in this legacy for our future begins with your example as a parent and how you take care of yourself.

THIS IS A CALL TO ARMS

I urge you to treasure all that is holy and sacred in your parent endeavor. Let's take up arms of love against being a parent by default, living in fear and anxiety, and just generally feeling crappy.

You heavily influence the next generation of heroes. Be the light that shines for your offspring on the path to "Infinite Joy." Give it to yourself first. That's the only way you can give it to anyone else and have your true will.

Say this out loud, "I am a superhero!"

You see, your negative reaction to what your offspring is doing stresses you and makes you and them sick, which leads to premature aging, chronic disease, and early death. (Just because your child is an adult does not mean your stress magically disappears.) Most stress and chronic diseases are preventable.

Fortunately, peace lives inside you, from your Deep Joyous Subconscious Core to your fully aware, waking self. Your goal is to bring that peace to the forefront and have it dominate your life. Doesn't that sound wonderful? You can do this.

A calling to parent, in the context I'm speaking of, is a strong inner impulse toward being the best parent you can be, especially when accompanied by the conviction of divine influence. You are called by God to oversee the development of God's progeny.

The conviction of divine influence sets you free. Divine influence is where peace is. Peace lies in knowing the part of you that is connected to God ushers in ease.

Your endless worry and mind noise keep you up at night. Allowing divine influence helps you rest, night and day. Preempt that noise by knowing you have the power of the Universe working on your behalf. Rest easy and sweet in that knowledge.

That you possess this power is something you have forgotten about yourself. It's time to remember. Parent peace is the result of understanding parenthood as a calling from Source.

FINESSE

Ease lends itself to finesse. Let intricate and refined delicacy characterize your ease, your finesse. A mother was rushing to get to an appointment. She had her nine-year-old son with her. He did not want to get out of the car and go in with her. He dragged himself out of the car, dragged his feet, whined, and refused to move faster as she begged him to "Come on." She was continuously cajoling and begging him to come on. As I walked past her, I said, "Just keep walking." She stopped begging and started walking. After a few seconds, he stopped his whining and ran to catch up with her. Finesse.

Being a parent is more than you think it is. Practice stopping your mind. As an exercise, check every hour to see that your mind is quiet, especially when with your offspring. Your goal is to be in quiet mind at all times. *That* is where the magic is.

You need your mind to create, also known as work, and to solve problems. That's all. Have a quiet mind the rest of the time. Reside in the joy and peace resulting from this exercise.

SUMMARY

Knowing that what you want is ultimately being handled by the connections in your Deep Joyous Subconscious Core makes being a parent easier. Understanding this lubricates the finesse that makes being a parent fun. Hang out in "The Deep."

EXERCISE

1) What do you feel after stopping your mind consistently?

____

____

____

____

2) Which responsibilities weigh most on you? How stressful is each?

____

____

____

____

3) Which stressful feelings would you like to get rid of first?

____

____

____

____

Chapter 2

RELAXING INTO A PARENT MINDSET

"The fishermen know that the sea is dangerous and the storm terrible, but they have never found these dangers sufficient reason for remaining ashore."

~ Vincent van Gogh

The last chapter was about being a parent as a calling. Now we'll get into the ease of answering this call.

WHAT STORMS ARE YOU AND YOUR FAMILY WEATHERING?

Isn't parenting similar to the quote above? We brave the inevitable chaos and stress, throwing caution to the wind when it comes to being a parent. Once a parent, it's full speed ahead. When most people find themselves parenting, they are resigned to seeing it through. The many storms in family life swell and dissipate one by one. Sometimes they come continuously, but they finally ebb. We weather them all.

For instance, the holidays may pressure you to spend money you don't have, causing you and your offspring stress. Social and economic peer pressures are part of the great nonsense you let ruin your feelings of peace and well-being. Why do you allow this pressure to win? Let's not forget the individual storms your offspring go through. Have you considered their problems feel like storms to them? The deep lessons you can teach them (how to handle money, for example) to relieve these pressures can serve their health and happiness for the rest of their lives. Have you mastered the lessons yourself? How do you avoid peer pressure? Learn to protect yourself and teach your children to protect themselves where you and they can.

How do you relieve the pressures and unnerving consequences inherent in caving to peer pressure, money pressure, etc.? A way to preemptively strike and eliminate or significantly reduce future problems is to take a deep dive into your meditation practice and get in touch with the part of you that doesn't need the approval of others, the part that brings forth the overflow of abundance, the part of you that attracts harmony, cooperation, and peace. Are you in touch with this part of yourself? Yes? Then teach it to your children.

What if you could glide along the edges of chaos and dissolve its energy from a calm vantage point? Can you see how this would calm the emotional seas of your family life? Your health and happiness are found here. Many parents come to accept chaos as normal...and it is, but you don't need to let it stress you out and negatively affect your health, happiness, and longevity.

PARENT MINDSET

When you were single, were you afraid that after you married, your life would be devoured by parenthood?

Myth: Raising children is all-consuming.

Truth: Raising children is an extension of yourself.

Many are concerned that raising children will be all-consuming, devour their lives, and destroy their independence. Claustrophobia envelops them when they think of all the responsibility parenthood brings. They cherish their freedom and relatively carefree existence. Just as the universe is always expanding, you, too, as part of this great universe expand. Parenthood is a high calling and expands your greatness. You expand in many ways, obviously: physically, intellectually, spiritually. As a parent, it's a combination of all three with consideration for another person(s).

Physical expansion means...well, there are at least two of you now, right? Intellectual expansion means parenthood can sharpen your mind quickly. Spiritually (I'm lumping emotions and spirituality together because they are quite related), no greater love (spirit) exists than the love felt in the family unit. The emotions literally swell from the spirit and render one helpless with unconditional love and the glow of divinity. When the high of all these feelings levels off, you are thrilled to be consumed by it. You can scarcely remember what your life was like before. You're bigger, fuller, deeper, and as author Elizabeth Stone once said, "Watching your heart walk around outside your body." It's a profound experience. It calls you to be the best you could possibly be. It's an experience that, though challenging, makes you happy and proud when you are equal to the task —and you are.

Examine your view of life through your own eyes as a child. Open the lines of communication with your inner child with compassion and quiet reflection.

MY PARENT STORY

In 1987, as I was running myself into the ground trying to make my real estate business work, my marriage crumbled, and I fell into the depths of despair. When I look back, neglecting myself and my feelings was the last thing on my mind, but now I see it was the obvious thing that brought me crashing down. As I was walking down the street, near homelessness, picking up cigarette butts to smoke, in addition to realizing this was the legacy I'd be leaving for my son, I saw how woefully neglectful I had been of myself. I decided right then and there to put myself first.

Since then, I have:

1) A son who loves me and tells me I'm the best mother he's ever had.
2) Local, national, and international TV and news media coverage of my business.
3) A business that helps Black women and Black mothers, especially in their mid-fifties (because parenting never ends even when you have adult children), recover their power, and parents (at this point especially Black parents) eliminate the stress and aggravation of being a parent.

Some of us feel we are in some type of parenting prison. My experience taught me the process of breaking myself out of the *feeling* of being in parent prison. When I had to leave my husband and become a single mother, I wondered how I was going to make it. It stands to reason that my first order of business was to *feel* better. I did this through meditation.

PARENT HELL

Where are you right now? Are you stuck in parenting hell? Is your energy drained and your mind fried to a crisp? I knew that feeling well. As a single, separated, and then divorced mother, it was all I could do to keep from yelling at my son every moment. Hell, I didn't have the energy. My negative experience was born from having too many expectations about the way it should be. I'd watched too much TV and seen too many commercials depicting the "Happy American Family," and I expected my life to fit into those pictures. My mind loved the cliché of the little cottage with the white picket fence, green lawns, bucolic landscapes, and the loving, lustful, bread-winning husband.

Real life showed up and said, "That's not what you've set up." Apparently, more was required. Watching TV and reading romantic novels is not a plan. Having a man is not a plan. I needed to snap out of it and fast. The well-being of my little son demanded it. What began then was the long journey from ignorance to bliss—the journey I endeavor to help you navigate. I ask you where you are on this path. If you will allow it, I will meet you there and help you cope and then thrive. My two degrees from The University of California, Berkeley were of no use in this area. Being a parent required me to dive into areas I had not studied.

I was in hell and didn't even know it. I was too tired to know it. I was working sixteen-hour days with my eyes firmly on the carrot dangling from the stick being held by the sales managers at the real estate firm I was part of. It was 1987. I was determined to "make it" so I could make up for lost time and "everything else" I lost in my divorce. I fell into near homelessness and depression instead. Loving friends kept me from complete homelessness.

I wanted to be a hero to my son and give him everything I thought he lost with the absence of his father. (I now understand that was impossible.) Time marched on, my son turned twenty, and foundation-laying time was over. It was the dusk of heavy mother influence. By this time, my son was quite sick of me. Too much bossy mom, too little proud mom. He was beyond full of mom-ness. Time was running out for me to make it all up to him, to make it all up to myself. I felt intense stress (which I now recognize as PTSD), fatigue, and self-defeat.

As I cried myself to sleep one night after being insulted by one of my supervisors at work, I remembered my spiritual practice. I stopped the treadmill. I realized all I had done over two decades *made me a hero*. I recognized that in myself. I had and have:

- Exhibited courage in the face of ongoing adversity.
- Gotten a Black male to adulthood in the US without him suffering incarceration or police brutality and instilled in him fine personal qualities, high moral principles, and high ideals.
- A son who now says I am a great mother and did a great job.

You are a hero as well. Are you:

- Still working hard rather than creating?
- Taking care of grandkids, adult offspring, and/or aging parents?
- Powering through health issues, fatigue, and worry?

You see, my hero, what you want comes in the "Gap of the Extremes." You want out of:

- Hell and the feeling of being in prison, and you want all of heaven and freedom.
- Debt, depression, and arguing, and you want all positive outlooks, peace, and joy.

- Feeling helpless in looming health issues, and you want to know you have a powerful say in how your health goes.

To get from here to there, you need to assess your position and move through the paralysis and disappointment to meditation, relief, and surrender. I'm not talking about surrender as in giving up. I'm talking about surrender as in surrendering the wheel before you drive into a wall.

You were not born to be mediocre, someone who just goes along to get along, blown in any direction, at the mercy of the whim of others. If you are using your power to choose sad circumstances, use it now to free yourself and your family. For my part, I am honored to serve in expanding your and your family's happiness and joy. You can give your child(ren) and yourself no greater gift.

FAMILY HISTORY DIRECTS FAMILY LIFE HELL

Family history (legacy) is a very important influence on how you behave in your relationships with your child(ren) and co-parent (if you have one). It's not pure genealogy here, because it influences adoptees too. This influence is about one-on-one interactions with your parents when you were a child, your grandparents when your parents were children, and on and on back through history. You see, what's happening now is a direct result of what happened in the past. You may be reacting to it in a positive or negative way. The influence of your history is still the profound driving force of your reality. Look at yourself and assess where you are on that evolutionary scale. If you are still having negative, knee-jerk reactions to various situations in your family, it's past time to change.

Do you object to making lasting improvements, life-changing enhancements, and leaps in "the thrive factor" for yourself and your family? Your family life and your individual life are deeply intertwined. Once you give birth to a human, you are forever changed at the core of who you are and how you see yourself. You change at that moment into a divine caretaker, governor, and inspiration. Your assignment, should you choose to accept it, is to thrive and shine as you have never done before.

Hell is a relative place. If I were to attempt to run a marathon right now, I would be in hell within thirty minutes of starting, yet people run marathons (twenty-six miles) every day somewhere in the world. Being a parent is much the same. It is a grand, glorious endeavor that is generally taken for granted. The reality is it's a freakin' relationship marathon. Proper training is an excellent idea so you and your child(ren) get the most out of the experience; otherwise, disaster awaits, and it can wear on the very fiber of your nerves for years on end.

PRESSURE GETTING YOU DOWN?

"The Universe has chosen you! The help wanted ad reads: …
Willing to play long hours in the name of high service and

enlightened life performance. Compensation is unlimited peace, well-being, abundance, fulfillment, and love for you and all whom you touch. Position begins now and always."

~ Dr. James Rouse, Author

Pressure of all kinds can get you down. The exertion of force (pressure) on and from your mind causes many a health crisis and eventual death. Dealing with pressure, for lots of parents, is a full-time activity. This heaviness can pass from you to your children if you are not careful. Social pressure (a term I associate with adults) and peer pressure (basically the same thing, but I associate it with kids) to me are *subtle forms of bullying*. From a practical standpoint, this type of thing is *fed by your own energy*. Understanding that first and foremost goes a long way toward actually curing, solving, and/or dissolving this pressure.

Pressure is self-imposed. When you teach your kids this basic idea, it can waylay a lot of fear and sleepless nights for you and your children. How do you stop feeling pressure? Take your foot off the gas. Relax and know all is well.

Teach your kids how to meditate. Have them tap into the silent part of themselves that makes everything happen and makes them smarter. Tap in, revere the silence for a while, and then visualize the desired outcome. Let go, let God (the Universe, Allah, or however you identify our Source), and take appropriate actions with joy. This is the single best thing you can do.

Ignoring the call of joy from your core yields a disgruntled parent. Do you hear the call? If you are feeling unhappy in any way, that is the "call." The feeling is the call. Meditation puts you in touch with your joy. Teaching your children to meditate puts them ever more in touch with their joy and teaches them how to cope with difficulty. Do you meditate with your child? I started meditating with my son when he was about four.

Some years later, as I was yelling at my son, it occurred to me I had become everything I hated about my mother. I truly appreciate you for taking the time to take action toward being a better parent. This book is for parents whose number-one priority is their family life. Family life was my number-one priority when my son was born and even before then, but the programming of my own childhood seeped in and I saw myself becoming everything I hated about my own parent. She was a single mother, and I became one as well. I understand her pain much better now.

As I hit deep emotional and financial lows, I had very little joy and happiness in my handling of the parent experience. I set out to remedy that and did. So now I share my findings and experience from thirty-eight years of finding peace as a parent with you. You're welcome.

Your child listening, discipline, respect, the energy of money, and enhancing your family system are addressed as we progress through this book. Do the following three things before or after you engage each chapter:

1) List your fears (as a way of staring them down) and eliminate them.
2) Engage deeply and consistently in meditation. Use the form of meditation you prefer. There are many.
3) Consciously visualize and feel what you want your family to feel like and be. (More on this later.)

Use and integrate these exercises into your daily family life. Work at your own pace. Most importantly, you need to get rid of *fears*. The pace of doing that varies from person to person. Fears are only to be uncovered and eliminated. Don't linger in them. Some are deeper and may require additional help. Fear is the greatest obstacle to peace and parent proficiency. When you're feeling unhappy, ask yourself often and listen for the answer, "What am I afraid of?" As you go deeper into self-discovery and your fears rear their ugly heads, see them and begin shedding them. I want you and your family to be rid of them as soon as possible.

Let's jump-start the peace process with a meditation. The objective is to become silent and stay silent the best you can throughout the day (short of doing your work). Miracles live in the silence. Your continuous homework is to do a silent meditation three to four times a day. Ideally, meditate:

1) Before rising from bed. Don't fall back asleep. If you can't do it without falling back asleep, sit up and do it. (20 minutes)
2) Before lunch. (5 to 20 minutes)
3) Before dinner. (5 to 20 minutes)

4) Before you fall asleep: Keep it short; you don't want to get energized at sleep time. (3 minutes)

Remain in the silent part of meditation as long as you like with a minimum of five minutes to up to twenty minutes as your beginning guideline. When I started, it used to take me twenty minutes just to get to silence. The length of time you meditate is arbitrary. If you are clear/ silent in mind and at ease in 90 percent or more of your moments as you go about your day, that is meditation. Making a special time for it is not necessary if you have that.

The following is my favorite basic meditation process. I learned it many decades ago from someone whose name I, regrettably, don't remember. Let's get your clearing process flowing. Get ready:

> Sit comfortably in your chair. Release any restrictions on your body such as belts, wristbands, tight caps, and shoes....
>
> Close your eyes. (Initially read and do as you read.) Take five slow, deep breaths. As you breathe deeply throughout this meditation, let your thoughts drift away. Breathe deeply....
>
> Let your thoughts melt into the ether. If any thoughts persist, simply bat them away.... Breathe deeply....
>
> Imagine a ball of light in the center of your brain. It's located behind your eyes, between your ears, and about the size of a plum.... Make it bigger....

Take this ball of light and slowly move it down your spine to your tailbone. Split it in two....

Move each segment down your legs to your feet. Let their comforting glow help you completely relax your feet. Breathe.

Slowly move the balls of light up your leg to your knees, and as they pass through your lower leg, use them to relax every muscle, tendon, and nerve.

Scan with the balls of lights down to your ankles again to make sure everything there is relaxed. Scan back up to your knees.

Hold the balls of light in your knees and relax every tendon in your knees. Breathe.

Now, move the balls from your knees to and through your thighs to your hip joints, relaxing every muscle and tendon as you go. Relax your skin.

Scan slowly from your hip joints to your knees and back with the balls to ensure all is relaxed in your legs.

Relax your hip joints and buttocks. Hold the lights there to ensure your whole buttocks area is relaxed. Breathe.

Rejoin the lights into one ball at your tailbone. Totally relax in that area.

Slowly move the ball of light up your spine to the base of your throat. As you do, imagine scanning rays of light radiating from the ball that form a disk. Scan your whole trunk area, relaxing every organ and cell in the trunk of your body as you go.

With the ball of light that now has disc rays, slowly scan from the base of your throat to your tailbone and back to the base of your throat. Slowly. Breathe. Pull in the rays.

Split the ball of light in two. Move each piece out to your shoulders and down your arms to your hands.

Completely relax your hands and every joint, knuckle, and muscle in every finger. Breathe. Relax your skin, all of your skin.

Move the balls from your hands to your wrists. Relax every tendon. Breathe.

Gently and slowly move the balls from your wrists to your elbows, relaxing every muscle and tendon in your forearm. Scan to your wrists and back.

Move the balls from your elbows to your shoulders, and relax every muscle and tendon along the way. Scan. Breathe.

Once back to the shoulders, relax the muscles, tendons, and bones there. Then move the balls of light to the nape of your neck, relaxing every muscle, bone, and tendon in your shoulders and shoulder blades along the way. Scan the shoulders to the tops of your arms and back. Breathe.

Rejoin the balls into one. Move them to scan your entire neck from where your shoulders meet to the base of your skull, relaxing every muscle, bone, and tissue along the way.

Now splay the ball again as you did for the trunk of your body. Move it slowly from the base of your neck to the top of your head, relaxing your chin, gums, teeth, ears, and eyes. Pause a moment in the center of your brain and then move it on up to the crown of your head. Breathe.

Scan down to the base of your neck again, and this time continue down to the bottoms of your feet to ensure all is relaxed. Slowly checking as you scan up, all the way to the top of your head, let the light gather and spill out of the crown of your head like a spout and let the "Fountain of Light" envelop your whole body, completely. Breathe.

Breathe quietly in silence for five to twenty minutes or more. No sleeping.

When you're ready, open your eyes, move your arms, and shuffle your feet. Pause for at least a minute there and come back into physical balance.

SUMMARY

Relax into the parent mindset by remembering how you felt as a child.

You are your child's hero because you guide them with what you've learned about being on the planet thus far. Use meditation to connect and maintain your connection to Source, and begin to teach it to your child(ren). Teaching your child to meditate will eliminate a lot of problems.

EXERCISE

1) How ready are you to raise children?

____

____

____

____

____

2) If you are a parent and were to start over, what would you do first?

____

____

____

____

____

3) Where are you right now in your parent experience?

____

____

____

____

4) Where in parent hell are you stuck?

____

____

____

____

Chapter 3

ACKNOWLEDGING FEARS, ANXIETIES, AND FEELINGS OF BEING OVERWHELMED

"There is a part of us that is committed to staying the same.... It may show up as paralyzing fear...or our non-conscious mind may just subtly distract us and we don't even realize we've been knocked off course until sometime later, when we notice things aren't getting better."

~ Brad Yates

The last chapter was about relaxing into a parent mindset. In this chapter, we will uncover the fears that make relaxing difficult.

Take a look at how you treat yourself. Have you ever thought, *I know I should treat myself better*? Do you know better, but you do things that aren't good for you anyway out of habit? Let's look at a few of them.

NO GRIEVANCES

A key point of this lesson is not to have/hold onto grievances. The finesse that springs from not having grievances is pretty fun once you get into the groove of it. Fear is a central cause of grievances: fear of not getting something, fear of something happening, fear of being hurt, fear of...whatever....

You hold a grievance against having fear in the first place and/or the cause of the fear.

Different levels of fear become grievances, and you take those out on your kids and other people—such as when you are impatient with your children. Lula was an impatient parent because her nerves were wrecked by the thought of how much time it took to train her little person to do things. She thought, *Why don't you just get it? Get it right now; learn it right now, so I don't have to tell you this again and again.* All of that tension was unhealthy and unnecessary. When she just relaxed and had no grievance about how long it took her daughter to learn something new, her daughter picked up on things faster.

CREATING YOUR HOME AS A LOVING, PEACEFUL PLACE

Where is your unbridled joy? As a little girl on the edge of toddlerdom, I remember being "in Joy" at all times. I basked in the feeling. Everything was fun. Everything was joyful. Then one day I noticed others were sad. I don't remember what they were sad about, but I do remember realizing they were serious about being very sad. I thought, *Wait a minute; they think this is real. They think this sad stuff is real. This must be what we do here. I'll play along.* I melted into feeling sad as well. Then I forgot what was really real. There began my spiral into the rollercoaster of joy and fear we so lovingly call life.

That is what's happening with your three-year-old. Do you remember that fall into the hypnotic sleep of being human? Everyone has done it. You accumulate a lot of fear along the way, some joy, but a *lot* of stress, aka fear. It covers our Joy. I've peeled away quite a lot of it and uncovered the "Original Joy," the joy that flows in unencumbered. I want to have more of it. What about you? I endeavor to make this a perpetual state of being for myself and others. Get serious about being in joy at all times. It's the only game worth playing.

Have a deliberate, loving space in which you teach your offspring. For example, if your kid is uncooperative and having a tantrum, what do you do? Simply stop what you're doing, hold them in your arms, and hold them close until they calm down. Let them do the pushing you away thing if they must, but hold them securely so they can't move their arms very much. They simply must get over it. Holding them helps their little bodies let go of that energy and calm down. You're doing this in a loving way to help their bodies discard the energy. They have a grievance, but they don't really understand that. That's annoying as hell if you really think about it. Some are born into this world with a grievance or fear that was created in the womb and possibly beyond. The mystery of our lives is not fully understood.

If you're the stressed parent of an adult, work on you—it's all on you, even if they live with you. Remember, they're adults now. Perhaps they don't live with you. All the better. But you are still connected. The benefits you receive benefit them as well. When you sit in meditation, they sit. That's the spiritual connection you have.

Fear recreates itself over and over again and intensifies negative outcomes. Get rid of it. Get off the fear roller coaster. Can you see how important it is to address your fears and get rid of them? Lift this pressure from your mind and feelings. You can do it. (We'll talk more about how to do it in Chapter 4.)

WHAT DO YOU PUT INSIDE YOUR BODY?

Are you killing yourself quickly or slowly? How much of your food is poison?

According to the Pesticide Action Network, each year, around one billion pounds of pesticides are used across farms, forests, and lawns in the United States. Around 17,000 pesticide products are in use right now.... Research reveals that only 0.1 percent of pesticides applied reach the target—the other 99.9 percent impact the environment.[1] According to homeopath, Rabbi, and practitioner of holistic medicine, Dr. Gabriel Cousens, "Vegetarian mothers have 1 to 2 percent of the pesticides and herbicides in their breast milk compared to meat-eating mothers."[2]

Why look at nutrition and the things you eat today? Our brains are of primary importance, yet I believe we take them for granted. Nutrition, what we eat, sets us up for failure and success. I want offspring and parents to respect the importance of what we put in our mouths and the effect it has on our brains, health, and happiness.

Nearly every chronic and devastating disease known has its root in stress in combination with what we've eaten or ingested in some way:

- What are you putting on your skin? That's another way of ingesting.
- What is the effect of diet on your perception of what's going on in your life?
- What kind of communications are you putting forth that are brought on by what you feel as a result of your poor diet?

"Let food be your medicine and medicine your food."

~ Hippocrates

1 https://www.panna.org/resources/pesticides-101/. Accessed November 13, 2023.

2 Personal interview by the author in the From Parenting Pain to Parenting Peace Telesummit October 11, 2017.

Humans have evolved from having the rickets and scurvy of yesteryear, and we're still evolving. We're living longer than ever before. However, our minimum *unmet* daily recommended vitamin intake is huge, and our immune systems are slowly turning against us. We're not getting the exposure to germs we once did. We also have more allergies and asthma than ever before, which were virtually unheard of when we were predominantly an agricultural society.

What are you allergic to? Do you know? Perhaps *that* is why you or your child are having problems concentrating…or whatever problem you're having. It's pretty easy to recognize a problem if you or your child has hives all over the body. It's quite another thing if you're not considering the effect of food, medications, or allergens on how you and your child feel and react to life. Organic food versus processed food is the big issue of the day. We want to eat organic, but cost is an issue. Processed food is cheaper and often tastier, but it makes us sick and kills us faster. Hmm, which one is really the most expensive then? Food is an important factor in your and your family's feelings, as is exercise and how much sleep everyone gets.

You know the saying about computer programs—garbage in, garbage out? Nutritious food promotes a healthy body and brain function. Healthy eating helps to relieve stress. Poor nutrition stresses your and your kid's nerves and brain, which can cause chronic emotional, mental, and physical pain.

HOLISTIC HEALTH

"Modern medicine, for all its advances, knows less than 10 percent of what your body knows instinctively."

~ Deepak Chopra

Health, aside from inherited birth defects, is the result of respect for and engagement in the activities and processes that lead to and maintain optimal physical performance and happiness. Too many of us think of our health purely physically and disregard the power of our spirit to heal. To poopoo the mind, body, spirit connection is to invite sickness and disease and leave a hole for the ego mind to do its mischief. It's just that simple. What is this mind, body, spirit connection? Going forward, I'll refer to it as the MBSC. You readily identify with your body, so I think that part seems clear. You think you readily identify with your mind. Spirit, though, is a bit of a mystery to many, and connecting to or with it seems like a remote possibility, *if* one believes the Spirit is real at all.

A healthy body and healthy mind help promote recognition of the connection to your Spirit. Your spirit, in turn, supports/promotes a healthy mind and body through communion with the Divine Essence, your Creator. It's sort of a symbiotic threesome. Let me ask you this: Do you believe in miracles? If not, how do you suppose we all got here? If we are an accident, as many insist is the case, then how do you explain the intricate workings of our bodies and minds, the earth and the Universe?

The Spirit holds our cells together. It holds the earth together. It holds the cosmos together. What would happen if you were to directly address the Spirit, the thing that holds everything together? What a prospect! What would happen if you were to deliberately attempt to consciously connect to it? That sounds a little redundant—attempting to connect with that which literally connects every cell in your body. Where do you suppose the disconnect is?

The disconnect is your mind distracting you from this magnificent Spirit within you. When you quiet your mind in meditation and listen to this silent part of yourself, you begin to heal in places you didn't even know were sick. Your health begins to turn around and improve. Insurmountable financial problems begin to be dwarfed by your recognition of true wealth, and they eventually disappear in shame. (Yes, meditation is the cure-all.)

If you believe in miracles, do you place a limitation on them? Many do. When you remove the artificial limits you impose on them, embracing and engaging the MBSC in ever-deepening consistency will help attain what you want. If you (or your family) are having health challenges, choose to engage the MBSC. Look carefully into your nutritional, physical, and medicinal habits. Increase the speed of your recovery by doing daily meditation. Mysterious illnesses are not mysterious. They are often simply an answer to neglect. Is it challenging even to consider all the healthy options and changes your family needs to adopt? Relax. Take baby steps. Adopt a new healthy habit every month or few months. Start with daily meditation. Your spirit fuses the mind, body, and spirit connection in healing.

REST AND SLEEP

Do you have sleepless nights? Ensuring your and your family's "sleep hygiene" is intact helps ward off misunderstandings as well. When I hit perimenopause at around forty-five, I began to have sleep issues. I never had hot flashes, even during menopause, but sleeping is a recurring, once very big, issue. I walked around holding on to the underlying stress of denying my own dreams and not knowing how to handle things. My hormones added insult to injury. I felt stress and fear.

According to SleepFoundation.org, common causes of insomnia include stress, an irregular sleep schedule, poor sleeping habits, mental health disorders like anxiety and depression, physical illnesses and pain, medications, neurological problems, and specific sleep disorders. I suffered with the first six of those. Also, loneliness harassed me. Not only was I trying to sleep with "rocks in my bed" as The Pointer Sisters so eloquently put it, but a true longing for the ever-elusive soulmate compounded my failures. I have a dear man who came to my rescue as a companion when my son was four, but he had no interest in a physical relationship with me.

Have you ever been in a room full of people and felt completely alone? What's that about? I'll tell you what it's about. Write this down: You are invisible to you. Fear has you covered up. It manifests as insomnia to keep you off balance. It's also fed by society. You then think there's something wrong with you. When you think there's something wrong with you, you go down the rabbit hole of endless mindfuck.

I know. I've been there. I've left there.

In some deeply spiritual Eastern cultures, three hours of REM sleep is enough. Easing the body and mind into deep rest (even though you're awake) for as long as you need is what's important. It was a relief for me to discover that. Western medicine is not the be all and end all of knowledge. Loneliness and aloneness allow the deep exploration of yourself. Your self is powerful beyond measure and requires all the exploration you can give it in many lifetimes without distraction, especially if you feel you need someone else to fulfill you. When you fully see yourself, you'll be impressed. No one else need be. Sleep and/or deep rest is the ultimate brain and body refresher and rebuilder. Visit SleepFoundation.org to help improve your and your family's sleep hygiene if sleeplessness is an issue for anyone in your family.

PHYSICAL EXERCISE

You're traveling on business. It's been a long day and a long flight. It's midnight and you check into your room on the twelfth floor of a hotel.

You've been having an issue with sleepwalking, but you're not thinking about that. You just want to get to bed. You drift off—it must have been for hours. When you wake up, you find yourself hanging by your fingertips from the balcony railing. What kind of shape are you in to be able to do that? (ha ha)

Respect exercise and the role it plays in your and your family's health and behavior. Too often, we take our bodies for granted and unconsciously abuse them in the pursuit of happiness. When I say unconsciously abuse, I mean many of us are not fully conscious of the role our bodies play in our and our family's behavior. For instance, I used to regard exercise as unnecessary. It was just something to do to manipulate my weight and body image. This attitude caused me to gloss over necessary lessons I could have been instilling in my son, lessons that showed the parallels between exercise and discipline, exercise and health, and exercise and the release of happy hormones in the brain.

How much do you understand about how exercise relieves stress and depression?

Dr. Andrew Weil, broadly described as a "guru" for holistic health and integrative medicine, says:

> Human bodies are *designed* for regular physical activity. The sedentary nature of much of modern life probably plays a significant role in the epidemic incidence of depression today. Many studies show that depressed patients who stick to a regimen of aerobic exercise improve as much as those treated with medication.

When I went through my stressful, deep depression during my separation and divorce from my son's father, exercise was the last thing on my mind—and because I was isolated (by choice because that's what depression does to you), messages about how exercise could help me simply did not get in. If they did get in, they bounced off pretty quickly because the depressed mind dictates what is received. The quality of my physical existence went down.

Have you ever noticed how good information you need and receive is rejected, but suddenly, it gets through years later? Do you value the prospect of having done a good job as a parent? The beauty is that in taking good care of yourself, you're teaching your offspring by example to take good care of themselves. You're essentially getting double the benefit. You're taking your kids along for the ride. Let your love for them prompt you to take better care of yourself. What better motivation is there? Doesn't this perspective make it easier to get the exercise?

What skills would you like to have that make motivation in this arena easier? Making sure your core machinery, your body, is operating efficiently is central to getting your job of life done. Though you may tend to focus almost exclusively on behavioral and image issues, it's foolish to do so if you're ignoring what your body needs. The body temple comes alive when there's light, love, water, air, nourishment, and strength. Exercise is a mood enhancer. Perhaps you can stop thinking of it as exercise.

Actor James McAvoy said:

> I like playing sport, and I like doing physical stuff. I like hiking and I like climbing. I do a lot. But I don't like the term "exercising." I feel like with sport, you're playing games. But with exercise, you're literally just trying to stop yourself from dying too young. It's weird.

The body truly contains all it needs to heal itself, but you must enjoy squeezing and hugging all the cells of it to show it you love it. Think of exercise—or playing if you prefer—as hugging every cell in your body. Spark the urge to do it. Set it up as a romantic date with yourself. How will you go about doing this exercise project? Walking, yoga, dancing (did you know ballroom dancing lowers the risk of getting Alzheimer's disease by 70 percent?), weightlifting, ball games, etc. are fun avenues to explore. While you're finding the sport and form of play you want, I recommend lifting weights as a necessary strength and movement activity.

Use the mindfulness of yoga in using free weights. Lift weights, target all muscle groups, and use weights that are too heavy for you to do more than ten repetitions on any one muscle group. The idea is to lift or squeeze until the muscle fails. If you can do the eleventh rep, the weight is not heavy enough. Lifting weights that target all muscle groups, about ten different exercises, can be done in twenty minutes.

Think about the health challenges you're facing or the ones your parents face(d). Heaven forbid your child is having them. According to the CDC, child obesity is on the rise thanks to poor nutrition, lack of exercise, electronics, and TV. What would it look like to raise the bar on your and your family's level of dedication to exercise?

Most parents engage in some form of exercise and encourage their offspring to do the same, but few parents have a built-in regiment for themselves and their families that provides consistency. Get in the habit of reinforcing what's good for you. You will perform your best as a parent, grow healthier right alongside your family, and produce more peace in the household.

Exercise goes a long way toward helping your and your child's brains operate as they should—relieving stress responses and getting centered for the task at hand along with prompting strength and enhancing sleep. Exercise helps you tremendously on all fronts. Play and have fun with your family. Get creative. Enlist the kids to help. They're full of ideas. What do they want to do? Charades? Twister? Table puzzles? Exercise mental flexibility and creativity with art, craft projects, games, and reading.

By the way, if you're feeling and thinking you can't exercise because of the distractions in your home, I urge you to embrace those distractions. Put your arms lovingly around them physically and/or mentally, and relax.

Engage the relaxation response. Think and feel this as you relax, whenever you relax:

Rest.

Enter peace.

Loosen your joints, muscles, and nerves.

Allow Source to induce…

Xquisite silence, noiseless mind.

The more you relax, the fewer obstacles you'll have to reaching your ultimate goals. Your good life speeds toward you when you relax and breathes love into everything you do. Relax and breathe love for as long as your children (or you) need to. You have time.... They will then be filled with your love and allow you to have some time. Grab the moment. Don't rush. Rushing through these exercises will produce stress hormones. Relax and breathe. There is really no need to rush anything. You're not going anywhere. What you want in life shows up faster when you're relaxed and understand relaxation is part of how everything works.

Let's start working through some fears:

1) Find a nice tablet or notebook to journal in over the next month (and possibly beyond once you see the benefits). Find a journal you'll enjoy touching and holding, with smooth paper, and get some smooth writing pens.

In your journal, list your fears and begin the process of eliminating them. Just sit quietly and make a list of the things you fear or have anxiety over. It can be anything. Pay particular attention to your triggers. What sets you off? What triggers bad feelings or knots your stomach?

2) What does your offspring do to trigger you? List your fears in parenting (and in general). Why? Because your offspring can pick up on your fear vibrations and absorb them as their own.

Writing your fears down on paper gives you a point of focus on the fear or anxiety. It helps open your eyes and mind to it and, often, to its solutions. Writing by hand rather than typing allows a far better connection to your Deep Positive Subconscious Core and all the levels of consciousness and understanding you have in between.

3) Once you've listed your fears, you can begin working on them. No need to try to eliminate them all at once. Just work on the one or two that are interfering the most at the moment.

Have you ever had a question about something, and as soon as you asked it out loud, the answer popped into your head? Same idea here. Your point of focus on the problem attracts the answer; the answer is often embedded in the question.

Focusing on finding what your conscious and unconscious fears are will allow them to surface so you can examine them and begin to dissolve them. As long as they can hide in the shadows, they can wreak havoc on your life. Expose them to the light in your positive mind and many will fade away.

The answers to *how* to dissolve them may pop in for you as well. Relax in a comfy chair and take some time with this. (We'll explore it more in the following chapter.) No need to do them all at once.

SUMMARY

It's important to recognize fear as the core of all of your problems. Once you recognize this, you can begin identifying your fears one by one and getting rid of them, thereby getting rid of your problems. You're not getting rid of fears that help keep you safe, just the ones in the way of your happiness and peace.

EXERCISE

1) What core grievance do you have that causes you to lose patience with your kids?

____

____

____

____

2) What fear is creating a negative pattern keeping you from having a loving and peaceful home?

____

____

____

____

3) What are your thoughts on your mind, body, spirit connection?

4) What will you change for the better in your dietary, exercise, and sleep regimens?

Chapter 4

SHEDDING YOUR FEARS AND ANXIETIES

"Nothing in life is to be feared; it is only to be understood."

~ Marie Curie

LIST YOUR FEARS AND ELIMINATE THEM

According to the National Institute of Health, 22.8 percent of adults and 8.3 percent of adolescents have a severe impairment linked to anxiety.

The Centers for Disease Control (2015) and the Children's Defense Fund in the "State of America's Children" (2014) report said, "Over 50 percent of parents have (valid) fears that their child will be physically hurt or bullied."

The Substance Abuse and Mental Health Services Administration (2020) said, "CDC reports that at least one in seven children have experienced child abuse and/or neglect in the past year and in 2018, nearly 1,770 children died of abuse and neglect in the United States."

How important is to eliminate your fears? Look at high blood pressure. Heart disease. Loneliness.

When my son was a little tyke, I worried about his health and safety. When he was a teenager, I worried about him possibly being bullied or ignored. Worry was everywhere. Fear seems to come with the territory of being a parent. Granted, you may have valid fears about your offspring being hurt or bullied, but what you may not realize is the fear itself attracts the very thing you are afraid of.

Also, the fear you have accumulated from your childhood and past experiences contributes to your feelings of overwhelm and fear.

Overwhelming fear causes you to strike out in impatience, overindulge in alcohol and/or drugs, and engage in various forms of child- and self-neglect. You'll find that I often include you and the children in the same breath because you are connected that way, by breath and blood.

According to author, keynote speaker, psychologist, and perinatal mental health pioneer Shoshana Bennett, PhD (Dr. Shosh), "15 to 20 percent of new moms have some form of Postpartum Depression."

Many parents think their fears are justified and there's little they can do about them, but really, they have the power to eliminate most of their fears and a lot of bad outcomes if they just realize they can eliminate them, tap into the power within, and allow that power to melt the fear away.

Of course, some deep-seated fears—like fear of public speaking, spiders, depression, etc.—require deeper attention. Those can be overcome faster in direct sessions with a coach or therapist. Many can be handled on your own.

ENGAGING DEEPLY AND CONSISTENTLY IN MEDITATION

"I don't blame my parents for my dysfunctions…
I blame their parents."

~ Richard Lewis

Your stress, if allowed to grow, becomes your child's stress, your family's stress. They then act out because of it, which causes you to be stressed even more, and the cycle continues—often getting way out of hand. Do you know passing on stress can continue for generations? If you still have minors, just know when they grow up, they become who they are based largely on their experience with you. It will be tempting to blame yourself for their perceived shortcomings. Banish the thought. For all of the molding and building you do as a parent, the fact remains you are merely the usher, the conduit of the future, as your parents were for you. The core 15 to 20 percent of who you are is not influenced by environment or upbringing.

How deeply do you blame your parents for your shortcomings? How much love for them has been sacrificed because of your upbringing and their lack of wisdom? In the final analysis, how much of who you are today is really your parents' fault? Adulthood affords you the opportunity to take total control of who you are. You can become any type of human being you want. Do you, as an adult, take responsibility for your life, or do you still, like a whiney teenager, hold your parents in contempt for all they were able or unable to do for you?

Get over it. Your parents were not perfect, nor were theirs. Maturity dictates that you don't blame the angels for God's work. The beauty of life is being able to expand in all directions once you reach adulthood. The trick is getting to adulthood. Some don't make it. Don't blame yourself. Love your humanity, warts and all. Tote that barge. Lift that bale. Turn that kid's cell phone off.

But I digress....

Many parents think meditation is a woo-woo activity, but it's really one of the central ways to regain peace, health, and if desired, wealth. Meditation is central to gaining the peace and ease needed as a parent. Many of us are so stressed we've forgotten how it feels to be completely relaxed (if we ever knew it). All parents of adults need to let go and let God. Actually, we all need to do this regardless of the age of our offspring. Did you know we arrive on the planet with fear and ego ready to blossom? Fear, because the ego comes with us. Ego, because that's how we differentiate ourselves from others.

Let's begin to clear those two by establishing your meditation practice. (If you don't already have one.)

Clearing yourself from fear, which is brought on by the ego, means to quiet the mind and gives you the great benefit of living a peaceful, happy life. If you suspect fear and ego are the same thing, you are mostly correct, except part of the ego is needed for intelligence and physical operation. The part of you that is "I" in the sentence "I am" is the core and most powerful aspect of who you are. When this I part of you is allowed to shine through, you radiate and produce what you ultimately desire. (You're doing it anyway, but in an ass-backward way if what you have is not what you say you want.)

Are you feeling crazy? Full of dismay or despair? Please know that buried behind your walls of flesh is a glowing light of power and peace waiting for you to tap into it—and meditation is your way in. Many types and ways to meditate exist. In this book, we will focus on the central, simplest way, which is to maintain a quiet mind and hang out in silence—in the silence is where we commune with Source. Quieting the mind is challenging at first but totally worth it.

Are you aware of the benefits of meditation? You may have even heard others say it helps you "feel good at all times," which is a side effect of meditation. Here's why: You'll find as you practice over some days that you are "smarter." You'll have insight into things that once totally escaped or baffled you. Solutions to problems come quickly. You'll have more energy. Why? Because you are tapped into Source. As your practice deepens, you'll begin to experience overt miracles. At that point, you will have found where the magic is.

In my twenties, my mind was so noisy I wished I could tilt my head and pour water in one ear to rinse it out. Meditation worked to gradually silence this noise. Later, when I was practicing meditation regularly and selling real estate, a question was put to me I had no answer for. The answer came out of my mouth, but I had no knowledge of where it came from. It saved the deal.

A protective energy field helps keep you and your family safe from harm as you move about the world. It's a good idea, once you're consistent at it, to have your offspring meditate as well. Age three to five is not too soon, and just a few minutes at a time is enough. They'll reap the benefits and become more cooperative in general. If you haven't already done so, begin with a simple meditation practice of twenty minutes per day and gradually increase the time if you can do it without stress, tension, or resistance of any kind (three twenty-minute sessions—morning, before lunch, and afternoon or no later than two hours before bedtime). If you're very stressed, consider building to an extra hour in the afternoon if you can. Go at your own pace.

Only fifteen minutes per day in full, actual silence is needed to help jumpstart having a quiet mind most of the time. In the beginning, you may find it takes five to fifteen minutes or more just to get your mind to the quiet part. Start with five minutes a day and work your way up to twenty. That's fine. The important thing is to begin to practice daily at whatever level. Meditation is a powerful path to peace and prosperity.

If your mind wanders or insists on being noisy, this is your opportunity to assert yourself and take control of it. Just gently bring it back to what *you* want to happen and bat the noisy thoughts away. If your mind is particularly noisy, thank it for sharing, tell it you understand, and you'll get back to it later. Focus into the silence. Send this healing silence to all the cells in your body.

Many people use music in the background to help in meditation. That's helpful for some, but I'm a purist, going for complete silence as I was taught in the book *Transcendental Meditation* by Maharishi Mahesh Yogi. You're free to do what you prefer in this regard.

The following is my basic meditation process, a conglomeration of different ones I've learned over the years.

Meditation exercise:

> Sit in a quiet room where you will not be disturbed by noise, pets, etc. Use earplugs or noise-canceling earbuds to help block outside noises. They're not absolutely necessary, but if your household is noisy, they are very helpful.
>
> Ensure your waistline is not restricted and there is no tightness anywhere from clothing, belts, etc. Take off your shoes.
>
> Sit in a chair, feet flat on the floor. Or do what is most comfortable. Lying down works if you're sure you won't fall asleep.
>
> Sit straight and balanced with your back supported. Balance your head—it weighs ten to eleven pounds—evenly on your neck and spine.

Close your eyes....

Breathe deeply and slowly throughout your meditation sessions. Breathe in for a count of six seconds, hold for a second, and then breathe out for a count of six seconds. Let's breathe together.

Breathe in—one...two...three...four...five...six.

Hold...one.

Breathe out—one...two...three...four...five...six.

Repeat.... Breathe in. Hold. Breathe out. Breathe in. Hold. Breathe out.

Know your Deep Positive Subconscious Core is radiating peace and unlimited power throughout your body and mind. Relax your body completely. Scan your body and mind for any tightness and release it. Scan it intermittently as tightness tends to return when you're not looking. Breathe.

Relax into it. You are naturally powerful. Release fear. Heal your body. What do the truly powerful have to fear? Fear attracts more fear. It's useless. Let it go. Breathe.

Grace and ease are central to your natural state. Dive into the silence of your core clear self. Your goal is to enter the state of silence and pure, positive thought. It's okay if you have gentle positive thoughts.

Breathe. Remain in silent mind as long as you want.

As you get deeper into your meditative state and your vibration rises, you may notice involuntary twitches, movement, or sensations in your body. It's okay. Breathe.

Breathe deeply and slowly. Come out of it gently when you're ready.

Doesn't it feel good to know you're putting an end to a potentially vicious cycle? Your family will thank you, and you'll thank yourself. We're all connected. You are improving your efficient functioning as your love radiates throughout every aspect of your life. You can't help but feel fabulous and manifest miracles daily when you feel the light of your divinity shining through in every cell, feeling intensely good every second—can you see how worry would eventually disappear?

HOW TO BEGIN ELIMINATING YOUR FEARS

Use your journal to list your fears and the ways you could dissolve or at least minimize each of them. Fear is an energy suck. It makes us tense and tired, slowing or paralyzing our progress in all areas. It makes us yell at our children. Our children then register stress and see themselves as unworthy.

Begin the process of eliminating your fears one by one. Here are three methods I've gathered along the way from various sources:

1.) Eliminate deep-seated fears in bulk by engaging meditation (going to quiet mind). Breathe deeply throughout your meditation sessions and practice breathing deeply throughout the day. This enlists the power you have within to gently melt fears away. It takes time in many cases, but it is quite thorough and you can do it on your own. You will feel better after each session.

2.) Sit down and think of one of your triggers. Choose specific fears one by one and journal to dissolve them, using one or more of the following methods:

- Close your eyes. Be there with it. Go back to when the trauma originally happened (was it in childhood?) and be there in detail.
- Be in the sights, the sounds, the smells, and all the feelings… then pull your mind out of the scene and observe. Let the sensations move, change, and transition out of your body. When that's done, tell them—the younger version of you that experienced the trauma—what they need to hear at that time.

Tell them things like, "It's okay. You got through this totally fine. I'm with you now, and I love you. I'll take over now. It's safe to let this pain and experience go." Hug them and let them hug you.

Then come totally out of this and journal about what happened in that process. Feel love for yourself as you journal. Repeat as necessary.

3.) When all else fails, if you have fears, anxieties, or phobias you cannot get rid of on your own, contact me and enlist my direct help through the use of "emotional resolution." In most cases, I can help rid you of a fear, anxiety, or phobia forever in a few sessions, as I am a Specialist in Emotional Resolution. According to Cedric Bertelli, the Founder of the Emotional Health Institute:

Emotional Resolution is not intended to replace or to be a substitute for psychotherapy because psychotherapy and emotional resolution have different goals. Psychotherapy aims at intellectual and emotional exploration, cognitively identifying reasons for certain thoughts or feelings. Emotional Resolution is based in somatic sensations to bring about the resolution of unproductive or injurious feelings without the need for intellectual introspection.

Free yourself from the constant negative feelings and fears for your and your offspring's sake. I know—easier said than done. But it's worth the effort because negative feelings can dominate your physical existence to a large degree and cause chronic disease.

A FEW ADDITIONAL WAYS TO ELIMINATE FEARS AND ANXIETY

You can do any of these in your mind; however, journaling helps tremendously because it goes deeper into your subconscious to access the triggers of whatever the issue is. Write at least one page on the issue, and if you would take the time, keep writing until you can't write anymore:

The Worst-Case Scenario....

Here is the questioning sequence. (Write *everything by hand* if you're journaling.):

1. State the fear.
2. Imagine the worst thing that can happen.
3. What if that happened?
4. Then what? Keep asking "Then what?" until you see and feel how your mind has exaggerated the issue to hold you in its grip.

[Some like to jump to death as a legitimate fear/what if, but living with fear is worse than death. It's best to let it go. Death is a release back into Source, so move along; nothing to see there.]

Flip It to Positivity....

Write what the fear is and all you want to say about it. Then flip it over and state the positive opposite of it and say/write twice as much about that, addressing all the negative points you stated before and restating them as positives. Identify with the positive opposite because it is the truth.

Retrain your brain and feelings to flip to positive whenever a negative or fearful thought comes up. Three or more times a day pause and find three or more positive things around you or in your life. *Feel deep appreciation for each individual thing. Linger there.*

Relinquish Control and Surrender....

Turn the fear over to Source. Hand it over with joy and go about your business. Know the fear itself is separate and not real.

Fear is merely a crippling way you let your negative subconscious control you. Let go of the fear. Drop into your body, call it up, notice the energy of it, fully digest it physically, and pass it. Relax and surrender it. Let it go.

Journal about what just happened. Repeat as other related negative/fear energy comes up.

Feel love for yourself as you journal. Repeat as necessary. Journal at least one page daily.

SUMMARY

Let the grievances and fears go. You are often reacting to your offspring based on something that happened to you in your childhood. You react that way because you feel pressed for time and want to get busy doing something else. This may be hard for you to believe, but time is on your side. Relax.

EXERCISE

1.) What grievance is triggering your impatience?

____

____

____

____

2.) Are you afraid to explore your feelings and list your fears? If so, why?

____

____

____

____

3.) Name the one or two fears or triggers most often interfering in your life today.

____

____

____

____

4.) Which negative cycle from your parents do you see being repeated in the way you are with your child(ren)?

____

____

____

____

Chapter 5

INTEGRATING THE PARENT MINDSET

"We are tiny patches of The Universe looking at itself and building itself."

~ John Wheeler

WHAT IS THE INTEGRATION OF THE PARENT MINDSET?

Earlier in Chapter 1: Having Peace as a Parent and Chapter 3: Acknowledging Fears, Anxieties, and Being Overwhelmed, you embraced your calling and relaxed into your parent mindset by engaging peace in a deliberate way to ward off and eliminate all manner of fear and stress.

As theoretical physicist John Wheeler says in the quote that starts this chapter, "We are tiny patches of The Universe looking at itself and building itself." That's the big picture. It's very easy to become buried in what you feel is stressful and too much to do. Open your mind and realize you are an important contributor to the truly big picture, a picture being drawn by the Creator of Worlds. As a Child of Source, you are not working this deal alone. Unstress yourself and accept the relief and help that is there once you get out of the way. Engage meditation.

Below is an essay I wrote a while back that reflects the myriad concerns, myths, and worries I and many others struggle with in thinking about or actually being parents, the unsung heroes of our society:

> **Worry Gets in the Way**
>
> To you hero parents and want-to-be parents, your heart is in the right place. Getting your head and spirit right for parenthood is the most important thing you can do for yourself and your child(ren). What you want comes in the gap of the extremes between being totally stressed and/or depressed and living fully in the joy of being a parent every single moment. I get it. I've been there. We hold a spot in our minds where we know how it can be; we just can't seem to get there.
>
> I "knew" intuitively before becoming a parent that my "carefree" single and then my married life would be devoured by parenthood. I cherished what I thought was a good time and the freedom to come and go as I pleased. You see, I had helped my own mother quite a bit in the care of my little brother and sister, so I was in no hurry to do the parenting thing—been there, done that, or so I thought. I had been there all right, and I was *still* there. The roots of my parent anxiety had not been dug out.

Anxiety over bringing a child into this world in the first place is strong! I perceived this world to be a horrible place, so there was quite a bit of worry and handwringing over that. Every day in the news, I was reminded of what kind of "life sentence" I was consigning my sweet unborn child to. If it wasn't the violence of people, it was the violence of Mother Nature and freak accidents that sent me into fits of worry. I could see no joy in it. Why bring a child into this kind of world?

I worried about being smart enough or wise enough to influence a child's life positively. I was worrying in a vacuum, not doing any research, just worrying. I've talked to more than a few young mothers and would-be mothers who voiced the same concern.

Raising children is not all-consuming in a negative way. Your children are extensions of yourself and our Source as you are and ever-expanding. Parenthood is a high calling to expand into your greatness and recognize yourself as the hero you are. Heroes have a will and find a way. They expand themselves and their children in such a way as to be a light that helps improve the world. Strength and competence are the credo. You have the courage to do the right thing—that's the very definition of a hero!

Raising children is part of the circle of life. Why be anxious about bringing them here? This is their world, just as it's yours. They own it. We are all born to serve The Expansion of The Great Intelligence of The Universe. As bad as you may think it is, you're ultimately just another stretch of Cosmic Imagination.

Raising children does require wisdom, though, and the golden rule is at the heart of all the wisdom you need. I've spoken about the golden rule many times over the last few years, so much so I even crowned myself "The Golden Ruler" because I love it so much. Do unto others as you would have them do unto you can't be beaten as wisdom goes. If you would follow it even in the care of your children, many problems would simply fall away.

We'll now more thoroughly integrate the parent mindset so your peace is even more automatic. Let's start with the definition of "integrate." It is to combine one thing with another so they become a whole. The parent mindset is born in you when the child is born. You automatically want to protect, nurture, honor, and gently influence the child toward the child's individual greatness. Combine this parent mindset with your individual self. How one goes about this integration process is highly individual.

What's your parenting style? The four most identified parental styles were put forth in 1960 by clinical and developmental psychologist Diane Baumrind as:

1. Authoritarian (disciplinarian)
2. Authoritative (reasonable and nurturing)

3. Permissive (indulgent)
4. Uninvolved (child does what they want)

Your style may well be a combination of these. You decide which you are in any given moment. But which type are you most of the time? Which combination?

At the center of integrating the parent mindset is understanding your child's feelings at a given age because you remember how you felt when you were that age. This understanding helps you come up with effective, loving guidance. Having this understanding and compassion is key. Make a point of remembering how you felt at various ages.

Pull yourself together. You're not a perfect parent. Your parents weren't perfect, nor were theirs. The beauty of life is our children can expand themselves in any direction they choose once they reach adulthood. Will you be willing to let go once they get there? Practice now.

Children cause the light of love within us to glow brighter than it did before they arrived. Here's a little piece I wrote quite some time ago:

Glow

> Glow: a light emitted by or as if by a heated substance (your spirit), the warmth of emotion or passion, to emit light and heat without a flame, to shine like something intensely heated, to show emotion or elation.

> You, lover of your children, glow with intense affection and devotion to them. Sit for a moment (or five) and relish this very special gift. The glow itself is what energizes you and nourishes your children's emotions. You teach them their value with this glow.
>
> Sit with it and let it replenish you. Notice it, this gift from your children. Feel it mend the worn parts of you, ever galvanizing your reflexes for the joyous child-raising activities to come. There will be many....

How do you ensure you're ready with your glow? How do you keep the glow stoked? Engage in meditation even more if you feel the glow dimming.

THE GOLDEN RULE (TGR)

As your children are growing, I think it's important to teach them to "do unto others as you would have them do unto you" from the very beginning. I think fewer problems develop as you go along when following this rule because when you're showing them the golden rule daily, based on whatever's happening in the moment, it's easier later when they become teenagers with more advanced disciplinary issues.

Ask (and listen for their answer), "Is that how you would like to be treated?" Ask, "When you're on a playground and you see someone being a bully or being bullied, how do you feel about that?" or "What is fair?" Have conversations with them. When kids are helped to understand the golden rule as soon as they can start to understand anything, it's a whole lot more peaceful as they go along because they want things to happen smoothly for themselves. Teach them they're putting out the energy they want to attract to themselves.

An element of the golden rule is understanding the part of *A Course in Miracles* that says, "Giving and receiving are the same." The giver feels good in the giving, and the receiver feels good in the receiving. It's the same good feeling. Volunteering helps bring this understanding home. Teach your children to feel free to give without hoarding because they think they'll get less. The hoarding kind of thinking restricts the good stuff that's coming to them. This flow is a spiritual aspect of how things work.

Think of the movement of water in a river. A dam could be placed to stop the water from flowing, right? Then the water starts to back up on itself. That is what happens with your energy when you decide to stop giving; *your* stuff gets backed up. You can't receive your stuff because you're holding back stuff that it is best to allow to flow to someone else. If you just let it flow, you make space for what you want to flow in and everything is mellow. Your flow out is giving (doing unto others) whatever it is you're giving; giving clears a space for what you want to flow in (as you would have done to you). There are no voids in nature. If you can't receive, you have a block/dam.

Also, what you're giving is the same. If you're giving time, you suddenly have more time to give; if you're giving money, there's more money to give. It's a spiritual principle—the continuous flow without a void, like the ocean. You don't have a giving situation without a receiving situation. You can't pull them apart from each other. They're the same thing. If I'm handing you something, you are receiving it. Can you see when that's happening that there is a joining there? It is the same thing that's happening with the golden rule—it's a flow.

Start by recognizing giving and receiving are the same. As you train a child, the idea is to teach them to understand this so they don't fight over things. This is what's wrong with the adult world. For example, all the wars we have going on are useless. We're fighting over something we don't and can't even own. Governments are trying to own something they can't own. Think of it from the Native American perspective. "What do you mean you want this land? This land belongs to everyone. You're crazy."

Because we think we can own land, we have conflict trying to own something that belongs to everyone. We're all here on one earth; we're all standing on the same soil. How do we own anything? We can all enjoy what's here. It's what we want the kids to understand instead of fighting over stupid stuff. Kids tend to argue and get bullied over stupid stuff. Bullies have problems because of some blockage—there's no flow there. Something they needed—in terms of love, understanding, affection, or being heard—got ignored.

You're in a situation where you're trying to own something and hoard something, and it creates a tight spot you need to protect and surround. It creates tension, like a dam in front of a river. It's the same idea.

I think if we could all somehow get around this idea, wars would cease. Forgiveness would rule because we would see the pointlessness of it all. These blockages are the core reasons we have conflicts of any kind. So, if we start with the children, as we move through time, there'll be less and less and less conflict.

What's the cost if you don't teach children the golden rule? The cost is reflected in the world we live in. The golden rule is nearly completely invisible. The big picture is obscured. The wars, the killing, people thinking it is proper policy to kill someone, are misguided. If we ask most people how they feel about being killed, they're not crazy about the idea. How could it be okay to kill anyone if we don't want to be killed? Mothers don't want their children killed. The cost is misery.

Paying attention to the golden rule applies to children and relationships. In relationships, you want to receive certain things. If you understand what you're giving, it will make it a lot easier to receive what you want. That goes for children and adults—it is not something that stops because someone is an adult.

Paying attention to the rule is also a way of understanding what is being reflected back to you and why. Reflect on the golden rule, seeing in your child's reactions what you've given them—you're projecting what you received, and they're mirroring back to you what you're putting out to them. It is a matter of the golden rule mirroring and reflecting, and it applies to what parents give to kids and to each other. We all are mirrors of each other. If you see something irritating in someone else, in this case your children, it's a good idea to stop and look to see where you yourself are feeling or have felt that and projected the feeling onto your child. They are just reflecting it back to you.

In this whole idea of raising children, we need to stop and think before we react most of the time. We're so busy being on automatic that the deep knowledge we all have often just goes out the window. If you don't recognize this automatic mode reflects what you're doing with people, you just kind of walk around blind. It's like looking in the mirror and not seeing a reflection. When you look in the mirror, you see your reflection. When you look at others, see your reflection.

I see the beauty of myself reflected in you. If I'm in a bad mood, I see the ugliness of myself reflected in you. I'm more likely to want to attack you in some way or be unpleasant to you. We are just walking mirrors.

Ignoring this fact is why there are wars, divorces, people marrying the wrong person—if there is such a thing as a wrong person. I think it's just a matter of being in touch with ourselves and what we are attracting. We're attracting what's going on with us at the time. They're not the wrong person at the time. We attracted that, so it was what was going on with us at the time. The cost is unhappiness, pain, and suffering when we're not tuned into *ourselves*. Ultimately, all any of us want is happiness. Everything we do is about being happy. Make a point of being happy most of the time (yes, you control that) and see what you attract.

How well do you integrate the parent mindset with your individual self?

SUMMARY

You are the role model of compassion by showing your offspring the benefits of a loving attitude and integrity. Do you feel it, show it as an example for them, and talk about it consistently? Your role as a primary influencer is nothing short of heroic.

EXERCISE

1.) List your family priorities and the core values you want to instill in your family and live by.

____

____

____

____

____

2.) Revisit yourself as a child and journal about how you felt at different ages and in different circumstances and stages of life. Practice feeling and understanding what to do from your child-self when engaging with your child. List a few things here that you will do differently based on this perspective.

3.) What is your parenting style?

4.) What do you do that expresses your parenting style or combination of styles?

Chapter 6

APPRECIATING WHAT YOU HAVE

"Learn to appreciate what you have before time makes you appreciate what you had."

~ Anonymous

In the preceding chapter, the focus was on the integration of the parent mindset. In this chapter, we consider the outcomes of the parent experience.

PROOF YOUR KIDS DON'T MATTER

That's right. You read that correctly. Our kids, our children don't matter! They are annoying and distract us from our cell phone, laptop, iPod, TV, games, sports, and countless other things that are more important and interesting.

If you recognize yourself as this distracted, preoccupied person (be honest), you need to stop behaving like your kids don't matter.

Think about it. Driving falls into the same category. You gamble with your life, your kids' lives, and the lives of everyone else on the road for the sake of the cell phone. But you're a multi-tasker! Tell that to the 3,000-plus who die each year from cell phone-related car crashes. Your children are watching you do this. You're programming this behavior into them. They will grow up and do what they saw you do—then what happens?

Also, it's more interesting to be at work. Work is certainly more important than your kids. Without work, how would the family eat, have shelter, wear nice clothes, or buy more than you can afford? Never mind the fact that when you're old, none of this other stuff (phones, cars, work) will matter. Hell, you may not even get to be old. Wait a minute, then. If you don't get to be old and squander the moments you have *now* with them, you (and they) will be truly screwed. Your child's self-esteem is tied to the quality *and* quantity of attention you give them.

Let's weigh this out again. When you get off work, the cell phone and electronics can wait until your child has had full face time in measure of at least twice as much as you would give the electronics. Driving—pull over to the side of the road to use the phone or better yet, put it in the trunk until you reach your destination (unless you have hands-free Bluetooth). Love crusted over in neglect becomes stale and lifeless, and your children's self-esteem suffers. Don't let this happen to you and your family. Get your priorities straight. As the facts state, "If you love me, you will prove it by giving me your greatest gift without me having to beg for it. If you love me, you love to give me your attention!"

PARENTAL PARADISE—YOU HAVE IT NOW

"Meditation makes the entire nervous system go into a field of coherence."

~ Dr. Deepak Chopra

Parental paradise looks different to different people—sort of like the definition of financial independence. The definition depends on the person. You are in parental paradise right now and don't even know it. Whatever the circumstances and experiences you are going through right now, it is exactly as you have requested, maybe unconsciously. I know, I know. Some people are going through some pretty rough experiences right now. No one wants to think they are asking for a mess or attracting hardship, but you are "made"/born to ask and receive. The asking may have been unconscious.

You create all the time. Looking back, I did a lot of unconscious creating. Fortunately, my mama put enough spiritual stopgaps in that I did not totally self-destruct. I think back over some of the things I did, and I know that by the Grace of God, and on more than one occasion, I was spared death. That was her doing. I weep at the beauty of it now, though at the time my lessons were being instilled at home, I didn't truly appreciate them. You know that drill....

Where is the paradise you want to be in as a parent? Is it with obedient and respectful children who do as you ask the first time you ask? Is it with happy, healthy children who love to do their household chores and homework? Perhaps they love sports and endeavor to bring home perfect grades because they find it oh so fulfilling to do so. (Wink, wink.) They're thoughtful, considerate, and volunteer at the senior center because, gosh darn it, it's just the right thing to do. They understand the golden rule and carefully live by it because you do. Sigh...so beautiful.

That paradise is possible, and some even have it, but what about you? Value the reflection of yourself mirrored by your child. It is how you see what to improve. In fact, The Universe, God, Goddess, The Divine, Jehovah, Ishvara—however you address Our Source—drives all progress and expansion with love as the power source. What you want is given when you remain in the center of your Power Source. Do you power through, stressing yourself until you collapse and make yourself ill? Is your mind driving you crazy? Parents, this bullying of yourself has to stop. It spills over onto the kids.

VISUALIZING THE FAMILY YOU WANT

"We (humans) process visuals 60,000 times faster than text. Further studies find that the human brain deciphers image elements simultaneously, while language is decoded in a linear, sequential manner taking more time to process."

~ 3M Corporation Research

Are you feeling somewhat better through your meditations? If so, in feeling better lies the chance to add some pictures to yield even faster results. Visualize what you want for your family. Engage visualization to help grab and maintain positive focus. Visualization of how you want things to happen is important for offsetting the negative musing visualization we all tend to do. Fortunately, it's all about what you want *now* for your future, not what you've done in the past.

Many parents actively engage their imaginations in worst-case scenarios that can happen to their family or offspring and dread negative outcomes, but really, if they would direct their focus and imagination on what they truly want for their families in every moment, they would see a significant contrast and improvement in the feeling and behavior of the entire household.

Over dinner, Marcus and Sherry recounted to me how far they'd come from debt, near bankruptcy, and yelling at their three kids by employing meditation and visualization. They had been fighting and considering divorce. At the time, as Marcus was searching for documents to assist with a possible bankruptcy filing, he came across an article I'd given him about visualization. Across the top it said, "What would you rather see?" Since he was at the end of his rope, he figured he had nothing to lose by giving it a try and decided to begin using the process.

A short time later, noticing the improvement in Marcus' attitude, Sherry began meditating and visualizing as well. In a few months, they had smoothed the edges of their relationship. Shortly after that, the nagging creditors simply stopped. Within a year, more money was flowing into their business to the point of excess. They were experiencing a much happier family life and were in the process of buying a home. I tell you, you are magic.

"In every situation that unfolds in every moment of our lives, we get to consciously decide whether we are going to focus on the outcome we desire or on the outcome we dread. With every thought and feeling we send in either direction, we are breathing life into one."

~ Christy Whitman, Author and Life Coach

Have you ever considered that everything you have is something you asked for, the good and the bad? Well, that's the truth. You practice visualization often, perhaps daily, and if you're not happy, the visualizations tend to be about something you want to happen but don't believe will happen or don't want to happen, and as a result, that thing you don't want shows up because of the kind of energy and attention you focused on it. Daydreaming is part of this. It's visualizing with our eyes open. We daydream about desired and undesired outcomes. What was the last daydream you had?

The bottom line here is: It's important to feel good at all times. Does that seem impossible, even unreasonable? Well, when you consider you create it all, good and bad, in the first place, it behooves you to be in charge of your thoughts and feelings.

Here's a simple formula for your visualization practice. Remember, it's not about trying to fix something in the present. The present is already done.

WHAT WOULD YOU RATHER SEE?

Get into your positive, meditative state of mind or at least a good mood. Then call up the image, the scene of what you want to see appear in your life and the feelings (extremely important) the image evokes. Add in all of your senses, everything that makes it real in the physical world.

Where are you? What are you seeing, smelling, hearing, touching, and feeling emotionally? What are the colors? How does the air smell? How does the air feel on your skin? What textures do you pick up with your fingers?

Are you warm or cold? What sounds are present? Who else is there? Add a few lines of loving dialogue. It's your movie. Make it come alive. Hang out there for a few minutes. Open your eyes (if they were closed).

Let's do one together that I experienced recently at a CEO Space meeting:

> Close your eyes (obviously open as you read this the first time). Breathe deeply throughout this visualization (and in life in general). Think of your family; connect to those you love.
>
> Focus on all of the things you're grateful for. Feel deep appreciation for them now. Love how all of these things have enhanced your life.
>
> See that you're in a meadow. The sun shines warmly on you as you smell the deep green of the flowing grasses being swept gently by the wind. Hear the babbling sound of moving water lofting over the tree-lined hill in the distance.
>
> The intermittent smell of roses wafts across your face. You look to your left and see the rose bushes and gardenias waving to you as if to say "hello." You smile and begin to walk toward them. It is simply the most beautiful scene of nature you have ever witnessed.
>
> Enjoy the beauty and connect to it. There are towering redwoods and oak trees reaching up into the blue sky as if they are antennas to Source. A wave of awe comes over you.
>
> You hear laughter coming from around a bank of trees to your right. You follow the sound. Your family is there, gathered around a picnic table covered in a beautiful cloth of your favorite color, loaded with all of your favorite foods.

> You feel intense love at the sight of them. They turn to greet you and you feel they are in intense love with you as well. You step to each one and interact with each lovingly and exactly the way you want.
>
> Celebrate. You celebrate with hugs with each step you take to greet them individually, feeling your intense love for each other. You sit and hang out for a while in joyous, quiet conversation with them. Music begins playing softly in the background, as you taste a bite of each delicious thing on the table. You feel so glad you're there....
>
> Now is a good time to gently open your eyes and come out of the visualization.

Feeling good? Now, go about your day or evening or whatever. It's good to do visualizations anytime or anywhere you feel safe. It isn't absolutely necessary to close your eyes.

Do you have a good feel for seeing the relationship you want to have with your family?

SUMMARY

Appreciating what you have in having a family and really savoring it will yield more to appreciate and savor. Be deliberate in what you create in your family. Engage visualizations to bring about what you want.

EXERCISE

1.) Where is your paradise? Please describe in the lines below what yours looks like...your parental paradise. What's on your list?

2.) How good are you at giving your undivided attention to your children?

3.) What have you learned about yourself from the reflection in your child's eyes or behavior?

____

____

____

____

____

4.) Can you feel the general improvement in your mood overall when you consciously visualize and feel what you want your family to feel and be? You know your circumstances best. What visualizations would you create for yourself? They can include your family or not. It's up to you. Create two or three or more over time on separate sheets of paper. As you get better at creating them, come up with ones to do with and for your offspring. Guide them in visualizations, like bedtime stories as they gently fall asleep. Outline a few of them here.

____

____

____

____

____

Chapter 7

GETTING WHAT YOU WANT AND PARENTING AT THE SAME TIME

"Dynamic activity and deep rest of the mind are complementary to each other."

~ Dr. Deepak Chopra

In the last chapter, we looked at appreciating what you have in your family. In this chapter, we will address how to get what you want and parent at the same time.

I love the quote above from Dr. Deepak Chopra. Dynamic activity (aka household, family, and business chaos) is not usually thought of as complementary to the deep rest of the mind. They are usually considered completely opposite, and they usually are, but the operative word here is "complementary."

Complementary can go a couple of ways here: (1) they can be complementary in that dynamic activity causes you to need deep rest, or (2) you can experience the two simultaneously. I interpret the quote to mean you can experience dynamic activity and deep rest of the mind simultaneously, which is the most efficient and healthy way to proceed in the chaos of family life (or life in general). In fact, the deep rest of the mind is a dynamic activity because during rest, you are in clearer communication with Source.

Do you feel parenting and getting what you want are mutually exclusive? Let's consider a few points of family chaos and stress for a moment.

As you see and visualize the family you want, you are the artist creating what others may deem a lie. This visualizing serves to help manifest the family you truly want. What kind of relationship do you want to see yourself having with your family?

The myths about parenting tend to lend an undercurrent of fear and dissatisfaction to your life. Myths like:

1.) Repetition, aka nagging, creates change.
2.) Raising children is hard and stressful.
3.) Parenthood devours your life.
4.) Anxiety about bringing children into this troubled world is justified.
5.) You're not wise enough to raise a child.
6.) Raising children requires too much money, and on and on.

These are all, what I call, mind-copulations. They have no basis in reality. They are all mental gas, things we make real.

The truth of the matter is:

1.) Positive repetition creates positive change.
2.) Raising children is only as hard and stressful as we make it.
3.) Our child is an extension of ourselves.
4.) The process is part of the circle of life.
5.) All we need is the golden rule.
6.) We have access to abundance.

These things are the truth, and the truth shall set you free. Your reality is fluid. You're creating it as you go. The challenge is to recognize your point of control and use it to make things the way you want them to be.

Parenthood was my wake-up call. I figured since I had purposely waited until I was older (thirty-four), mature, and married, I was ahead of the game. I wasn't. All the myths and fears I thought I had gotten away from in college and working on my own began to play out. I had no idea I was going to recreate most if not all of my childhood pain, the pain of feeling abandoned, hungry, poor, not good enough, and barely loved. I would relive the feelings of it all—and visit those same feelings upon my son.

Raising children is hard because of the childhood pain we revisit, the myths we buy into, and the haunting depression we walk around in. Adults perpetuate their own childhood pain, making communicating with the child an uphill battle and discipline a nightmare or non-existent. Saying or screaming something ten times or more is pointless and compounds the stress you feel. Sometimes we sense something's wrong but, like a zombie, we don't even know we are dead.

YOU AND YOUR FAMILY ARE NOT THE PERFECT FIT

You and your family are not the perfect fit. Just kidding. Of course, your family is the perfect fit for you and you for them. The Tao Te Ching says, "When the student is ready, the teacher will appear." This is oh so true in the case of parenting. Your child is sent to teach you specific lessons in love. As every child is different, so are the lessons. Ha! You thought it was all about you teaching them, didn't you? That's only half of the story. These lessons range from sweet and breezy to gut-wrenching. Your part is to recognize what you need to learn or fix in yourself—then learn it and/or fix it, preferably in short order before doing permanent damage to the child, physically or emotionally.

My son taught me patience and the realization on a very deep level that the world isn't all about me and what I want. I felt how broken I was inside and had a clear view of my short-sightedness. As much as I wanted to blame his father for my predicament, I had to own up to the fact that I had chosen this man to be the father of my child.

Perfection is overrated—you're perfect, then what? Seems to me decay is next. Perfect parenting does not exist, yet it is available to you because you are perfect in your imperfection. Your imperfection is perfect for the circumstance at hand, which is to expand or evolve into a better parent and person. Lessons children teach galvanize you into a stronger, more joyful existence and an ever-deeper love.

Know you are the perfect parent if you are doing what it takes to repair your broken heart and emotions in a timely manner. How can you tell what's broken? Start looking at the buttons that cause you to fly off the handle or get a sinking, sick feeling in your heart or stomach. Start to recognize the feeling before it is a full-blown reaction. Get this right and you can have it all: calmness, peace, and joy throughout the land and family.

FLIP THE SCRIPT ON YOURSELF!

Know yourself. Know why you do what you do. Know you are perfect when you are doing all you can to repair your brokenness. In doing what it takes to repair your broken heart and emotions, you will notice an improvement in your overall experience of your family. This may sound funny, but if you do this before you have children, chances are good you will attract child(ren) who are easier to manage. That could happen, and/or you could be substantially better at managing difficult children. You will be more patient in dealing with them. It will be easier on you and easier to inspire them to their greatness.

The quality of your attention is the quality of your parenting results. Listen with your whole body as often as you can. Things tend to get hectic. If you have a lot of background noise and emotion going on in your head and heart, you will miss a lot of what is said and totally miss important clues to what's really going on in your child's mind and heart. I recommend taking your own inventory: Were both of your parents in the home? Was their marriage a happy and loving one? Was your home life as a child happy? Did you feel extremely, unconditionally loved? How are your manners? Did you receive instructive, effective discipline without abuse? The answers provide a clue to possible issues that need addressing, issues of which your child need not feel the brunt. Seek to understand yourself, and when negative issues are discovered, nip 'em in the bud.

As a hero parent, you take your calling seriously. I didn't understand the path I was being called to at the time, but I do now. Do you?

A means for relieving anxiety is to tune into your thoughts and feelings and ensure you flip the bad feelings to good the moment you feel a bad feeling. I know it sounds easier to do than it is, but do it you must. (Sounded a little bit like Yoda on that one, huh?)

WISDOM REQUIRED TO RAISE CHILDREN

Truth: All you need is the golden rule.

People who give the subject serious thought sometimes come to think raising children requires wisdom they don't have. The idea has some merit, but it is essentially a myth. When it comes to showing children the best way to live and respect others, the golden rule is truly all you need, and I suspect most of us have this basic wisdom. I talked about the golden rule in Chapter 5 and I have talked about it many times over the years. As I said earlier, I even crowned myself "The Golden Ruler" once because I hold it so dear. This particular rule is essentially innate to our human intelligence—intelligence that must be cultivated, hence, being parents. You don't necessarily feel this rule as toddlers or children. At that stage, you're a ball of "mine, mine, mine" and "What about me?"

Think of all the conflict and suffering we could have avoided had the golden rule governed each moment of human history! We would have peace throughout all lands. No wars would have been fought. Love would reign supreme, and my little brother would not be the scarred creature he is today (just kidding). Our trust in the food we eat and products we buy would be totally warranted because we would know the people producing them created them as if for their own children, whom they love as themselves. Sure, there's all kinds of other wisdom to be had about how to treat each other, but I venture to say those are extensions of the golden rule. Other ideas and rules exist and are necessary because we do not adhere to the golden rule in the measure required for maximum happiness. Let's make this correction now. It's a tall order but well worth the effort to pass on these benefits to our children and their future.

YOU WANT TO STRANGLE YOUR CHILD

Do you sometimes feel like you want to strangle your child?

According to ChildWelfare.gov, more than 1,800 children in the US died from parental abuse or neglect in 2019, up from 1,660 in 2016. Can you imagine what that number is now, after the pandemic?

How often have you read or heard about a parent who went off the deep end? They've drowned their children, done away with the child and/or the spouse, or committed some such other crazy act to cope with "the big challenge," whatever it was. Trauma lives in the body and is passed on through the generations.

According to the article "Can Trauma Be Passed from One Generation to the Next?" at Psycom.net:

> Trauma can leave a chemical mark on a person's genes, which can then be passed down to future generations. This mark doesn't cause a genetic mutation, but it does alter the mechanism by which the gene is expressed. This alteration is not genetic, but epigenetic.

We can control these epigenetic expressions (changes in gene expression rather than genetic code). The stresses of raising children and trying to maintain a family make a lot of people crazy. A lot of unhappiness is caused by what we believe *should* be happening but is not. We create unrealistic expectations, some delusional, some peer pressure, and go off the deep end when stress builds up and things don't go "right."

I, for one, thought to myself many times, *If I have to say that one more time, I'll scream.* I think I did scream a few times—and not in a good way. I couldn't continue to hang out there in that whooping, yelling space in my head. It would only have escalated into more of the same and on to worse. Reassessment was in order. I'd lost sight of the bigger vision.

Life's many and varied issues can impair your vision of what's truly important. The consequences of allowing yourself to be carried away in the sea of stress and unhappiness include that your children will likely drown in it with you. They will receive and pass on the legacy of a joyless existence, depression, and pain.

Was this trauma passed to you? Is it what you want? You have the power to change it. You can remove impairments from your better vision.

Reverend Michael Beckwith believes when we want to change and believe the change will happen, we remove those impairments and create that better vision. He states:

> The Prayer and the Answer Are One. When you realize that your prayer and its answer are one, then you close the gap between prayer and manifestation. On the other hand, when you think that God will run errands for you, then you neutralize your trust in the fundamental goodness (aka Power) of the Divine by placing your good in the future. Your good is happening right now, even as you accept this statement of truth.

In fact, The Universe, the essence of which is God, Allah, Goddess, The Divine, Jehovah, Ishvara—however you address Source—drives all progress and expansion with love as the power source. You are part of that power. What you want is given (nearly immediately) when you *consciously remain in the center of your power source*. Remaining in the center of your power source is your true work (that word we love to use so much). Think of it as a *game worth playing*. It's how you actually create what you want.

YOU DON'T KNOW WHAT YOU'RE CREATING

You know what I hate? I hate the word work. That word suggests arduous, joyless, slavish activity. Oxen work. Cars work. Computers work. But humans create. Creative ideas are the domain and mainstay of humanity.

You are creating all the time. Everything you do is creation. Your work is creation. I think when people understand they're not working but creating, it lightens the emotional load for them. If you didn't think of it as working, if you really knew whatever you're doing is creating, it would be a completely different feeling. "I have to go create today." That's what you do, you create. If you're a janitor, you're creating a clean space; you have tools you use (created by other humans) to create a clean space. If you're a rocket engineer, you're creating a rocket that takes people into space.

Moms and dads (endeavor to) create happy family environments. Children (endeavor to) create good grades in school. Free apps found all over the place are created. You create what? How much happier would you be if you would just change that one little word? Right? If you cut the word work out and think of it as your creation because you're creating all the time, what you do would feel completely different and more enjoyable. You create bad situations; you create good situations. You create miserable situations; you create this situation. You are a creator.

If the approach in teaching was to enhance the ability of the student to create, how much more willing to engage would the student and teacher be? Bringing new ideas to the fore can be challenging. When students understand what was brought about before can help them to create or bring about even greater things, then stuff would get interesting. Vigorously support your offspring's creative ideas even though they seem weird to you at the time. I say we drop that word work. (Okay, you can keep it if it makes you feel good. If nothing else, I am a benevolent ruler.) Let's create away. Instead of "I'm going to work," its "I'm going to create!" Doesn't that just feel better? What are you creating?

YOU WANT CERTAINTY IN BEING A PARENT

As much as you want to compartmentalize the different areas of your life, all areas are affected by what happens in all others. They are intertwined. What happens in what you create at work and/or business affects your home life and vice versa. Your health affects everything. Your level of happiness affects everything. Children come into your life to inspire you to your greatness. That does *not* mean you are to apply more struggle and effort—quite the contrary. You are to relax more into the miraculous creature you are so you may show your offspring how to do it when they become adults.

I regret that with all of my waiting to be wise before I had a child, I fell into the same struggle and effort mindset that surrounded me. It's what most of us do. There is no final, ultimate wisdom to be attained.

You are evolving. I am evolving. It doesn't stop. If your child is having a tantrum, just let them do it. Don't give energy to it except to remove them to isolation if it's bothering you, disturbing others, or they may hurt themselves or others. Sure, your dinner or shopping was interrupted because you had to drop everything and leave, but chalk it up to the child needing to have their moment privately. No yelling, no screaming on your part, just quiet protection and an exercise in calming your nerves while they do what they're doing.

Parenting, one of the most important jobs in the world, is executed largely by people who have no experience in the job. Even if some think they are experienced, along comes the child who proves them wrong. What is your guide on this sea of uncertainty? Feelings. It's about feelings. Everything you do is about how you're feeling. How you feel dictates what shows up in your life. If you're feeling good most of the time, then mostly good stuff shows up.

Teach this to your children as you are doing it and as you are learning to do it. It enhances their and your experience of life to know how to keep your feelings at a certain good level. The things you want can show up as you want at this level, and there's a lot less frustration and need for heavy discipline. If you stop in the moment and check your feelings in a loving way, they tell you what you need to do. You can examine the thoughts that led to a bad feeling and change them. You can ask yourself, "What thought is going to put these feelings where I want them to go?" Push the pause button and reflect instead of being on automatic with negative reactions. In the moment is where the feeling is. Recognizing that is the difference between a happy life, an okay life, or a miserable life. How good are you at controlling your feelings and what you are creating?

WHAT DID YOU SAY YOU WANT?

What was on your list of wants from the Introduction? As you integrate the parent mindset (from Chapter 5), it will be easier to get what you want and be a parent at the same time. As the list of wants is highly individualized from one parent to the next, I set forth here the principal cause of you getting what you want (and don't want), whatever it is: knowing what you want and knowing it in an ownership way. To know it is to own it. When you own it, you have it.

EXERCISE IN KNOWING (YOU HAVE WHAT YOU WANT)

"Live in the feeling of your wish fulfilled."

~ Neville Lancelot Goddard

Know: To perceive directly; to apprehend immediately by the senses or the mind; possession of a fact in memory; have mental certitude regarding.

Knowing: attaining knowledge, cognizance, consciousness.

It's the spontaneous quickening of your knowing that causes the miracles you've asked for to suddenly (and gradually) appear in your life. When you are totally silent in your mind, what is happening? You are in a state of intimate, heightened sensitivity and receptivity with Source. You have access to all-knowing in those moments. Have them often.

Central to a lot of stress is struggle and effort (S&E). Counter to struggle and effort is the feeling of ownership. Inside the feeling of ownership is knowing (you have something). This doesn't apply to obtaining other humans, though, because, you know, they're Source as well. Your desire and theirs must be the same for you to "have" them. This knowing, also known as certainty, is what seals any deal for you. When you feel you know it, you feel clear on the subject. You take what you know for granted. That's how you know you know it: your name, your secrets, your capabilities—your child.

Here is an exercise for getting what you want (knowing):

1.) Choose something on your list and perceive directly with all of your senses; sight, sound, smell, touch, taste, feeling, that you have it. Zero out all noise and doubts in your heart and mind. Maintain this state at all times. Know you are Source as you are having it.

2.) Go to Silence in your mind (it may help to close your eyes) and place it there complete and done. Revel for fifteen to thirty minutes in all of your senses that you have it. The silence in your mind is the connection to the Source of everything you want and makes what you want happen.

3.) Go in again an hour later. Feel it complete. Visualize it for fifteen to thirty minutes as complete. What are the sights and sounds, things being said, by whom? What activity is being engaged? In the visualization, how is everyone feeling? Live it and visualize it as real and happening—because it is.

4.) Relax for fifteen minutes in "knowing" (feeling completely and owning) it is done. In this experience, feeling is knowing. It will be delivered when you are strong in the practice of your relaxation, knowing, then letting it go (because you know it will come about).

5.) Think about things you've received so far. Identify how and when you have already put any of the above processes in motion before. Celebrate and appreciate your power!

DIVINE RADIATION

You have tried cajoling, placating (and in the case of racism or any oppression, marching and fighting). It's time to bring out the big guns—Divine Radiation: The Love Force, a Love Undertow. Divine Radiation is what's needed.

Divine Radiation as a realization came to me after a thirty-two-hour period of prayer and meditation. It is the harnessing of the "Love Energy" central to your existence and sending it through space to soak into the hearts and minds of others to help heal them from all manner of destructive behavior: substance abuse, racism, violence, bullying, etc. Some of us do this already. This is the only thing that will free you and them forever. If you refuse to do it, you condemn your children and their children to continuing cycles of stress, lack, fear, and racial stupidity: racist, putrid hearts will continue the hate, and fear and lack will continue to rule and feed into themselves as self-fulfilling prophecies. The fear carried in our collective hearts has helped to perpetuate this darkness. As you know, what you focus on is attracted to you. Collectively, we have been focusing in the wrong direction for too long. It's time to eliminate this fear.

Rev. Dr. Martin Luther King, Jr. said it best, *"Darkness cannot drive out darkness; only light can do that. Hate cannot drive out hate; only love can do that."*

I dare say that participation in this "Love Force" will have additional benefits for you well beyond changing the hearts of people. Your health will improve, the health of your loved ones will improve, and you'll all be generally happier. This is quite a worthwhile side-effect. Many types of distance healing exist: Reiki, Amadeus, Tong Ren, Prayer. Divine Radiation is a mix of meditation, visualization, and energy projection.

Here are the steps to giving Divine Radiation:

1. Eliminate the fear this won't work (and any other fear you may have).
2. Get into a meditative state and think of someone (your child?) you love. Amplify this love powerfully. Feel it growing as a gentle flame burning inside you. Expand it to the maximum point inside you… then.…
3. Radiate the love, sending it out powerfully across the airwaves, through walls and state lines into the hearts and souls of all sick haters and racists in its path. Visualize it radiating from your heart powerfully in all directions. Do this also as a means of protecting your offspring.

Make this a daily five to fifteen minutes or more visualization exercise or prayer.

SUMMARY

Do you still feel being a parent and getting what you want are mutually exclusive? They do not have to be. You direct how you want your life to be, even with kids.

EXERCISE

1. How do you usually go about getting what you want?

2. How much "struggle and effort" have you done before now to get what you want?

3. Employ the "Exercise in Knowing." What are the various stages in feeling/knowing you encountered?

____

____

____

____

____

____

4. How do you know your family is the perfect fit?

____

____

____

____

____

____

Chapter 8

LEADING STRATEGIES AS A PARENT—THE LONG GAME

"Where attention goes,
energy flows and results show."
~ T. Harv Eker

The previous chapter was about how to get what you want and parent at the same time. This chapter's subject is the leadership aspect of being a parent.

When you create a legacy of having the courage to do the right thing, the will to create the family you want, and finding a way, you build integrity in your children and family unit. You walk the talk. You parent by example.

Have you considered the level and quality of attention required over the long haul of eighteen-plus years of raising a human? Sounds daunting, but it's really easier than it sounds. When you *harness your attention*, rather than allow the "shiny-object negative default" thoughts you have going on, you can make the long run easier and more enjoyable. Your major overall aim in the parent adventure is to lead your child into a happy, independent adulthood. Your plans of action in this endeavor really need to be more about you being happy, free, and independent than anything else, *so you can show them the way*. They see you doing it every day, and it's a given. To do this, you may have pain to work through. You may have deep-seated hatred to work through. You may have fears of all kinds standing in the way of the pure joyous self you need to be for your offspring and yourself. Address them now for the sake of your and your family's happiness. Let's look at a few strategies in this chapter.

CHILDHOOD AGONY REVISITED

As I think about adults perpetuating their childhood pain, I recall my own childhood. Looking back now, I see how very vulnerable and acceptance-seeking I was and still am, as most children are. Over the years, I've learned a lot that has helped me get over most of the vulnerability and acceptance seeking, but I still cringe at how inept I was in raising my son. You see, a lot of the sweet spot of child-raising-wisdom did not dawn on me until he was an adult! A tad late, I think, and a lot of dollars short.

My impoverished childhood, being raised by my single mother, younger brother in tow, had no room in it for new shoes and new clothing, eating out (we were lucky to eat at all many nights), Christmas presents, birthday parties, birthday presents, or fun paid adventures with friends. A stepfather entered the picture when I was eleven. Then life improved a little bit, but by the time I was in my teens, the emotional battle scars of not having enough, harsh discipline, and a cold-hearted mother had firmly fixed their grip. Only as an adult would I learn I looked too much like my biological father for her to love me or, rather, show the affection I so desperately needed. I'm sure she loved me.

Fast forward to adulthood. (She got me there.) Try as I did to avoid the pattern my mother set, I fell lockstep into every groove. The names and times had changed, but the love hang-over was the same. Yes, I was married, but it didn't last. It couldn't. I had no great example to follow. My college education did not include relationship training in its curriculum. My childhood pain was repeating itself and running me like I was on a runaway train.

Separation and divorce were a long, drawn-out process that had me depressed most of that time. I've come out of it, but when I was depressed, I was not apt to recognize or seek help. That was me. How do you behave when you're depressed?

Two decades later, my company Save Your Breath, LLC was born because I wanted to help other parents avoid many of the mistakes I had made over the years, and mostly, of course, to help reduce their stress factor. Though parenthood is one of *the* most stressful undertakings imaginable—blessed, but stressful—it is *totally* manageable and can be joyful with the right tools. I did manage to get life's most powerful core values instilled. If your offspring are still children, let's not have a bunch of crap to try to undo later. Varying degrees of damage can be avoided!

Strategy: Avoid corporal punishment and nagging (aka mental abuse). It damages your child's brain and emotions. Instead, stop in your tracks and relax; then see into the moment to discern what you both need, lovingly, and behave accordingly.

DEEP-SEATED HATRED OF YOUR MOM AND/OR DAD

"Any time your child pushes your buttons, he's showing you an unresolved issue from your own childhood."

~ Dr. Laura Markham, Founder of Aha Parenting

My mother had us starve the family dog in the backyard because when my stepfather would drive the dog far away to lose him, he kept finding his way back home. The dog had irritated her by grabbing and tearing the sheets and clothing drying on the clothesline. There was no money to replace these things he kept destroying. She'd had it with him. Poor guy was just having some fun.... What mark do you suppose this left on my and my younger brother's impressionable minds and feelings? We were probably thirteen and nine at the time. My youngest sister was only about four. I can't remember how many days it took for him to die; seemed like forever.

A question: How do you feel deep down inside about your parent(s) and how you were treated by them? Do you have a smiley face on it?

The world loves to see you love your parents unconditionally, and you probably do...except for that one little spot, maybe it's not so little. Maybe it's covered over with "understanding" and being a big girl, being a big boy. Well, you're an adult now, so if you were to visit that child inside you, you know that child would say and has said to themselves or even to your parent when you were a teenager, "I hate her!" or "I hate him!" or "I hate you!"

How many times did I think that to *my* mother? Too many to count and for varied reasons. I could never say it to her face, even as a teenager, because I liked having *my* face where it was. It suits me. If I had dared to say something like that to her, chances were good I'd be picking my face up off the floor! The point is you tend to pass this negative energy on to *your* children simply because you don't know any better. As Maya Angelou says, "When you know better, you do better." My mama was doing what she knew, what *she* received. She didn't know any better.

I followed suit to a large extent. Then as time passed and I learned how to do better, I did. Do you really want your grandchildren to be at the mercy of the negative or unconscious discipline *you* received as a child? Isn't it time to upgrade? Do you really think saying it a thousand times and sometimes screaming it is the way to go? What about corporal punishment? How corporal are you? Are you in a constant spanking/whooping situation? Are you out of control because of this deep-seated hidden hatred for Mom and/or Dad, or have you just given up and let the kids do whatever?

Strategy: Forgive your parent(s). Hatred eats the hater and, in this case, their young. No need to forget; just forgive.

ANXIETY OVER HAVING CHILDREN

Anxiety over having children in the first place is justified, but the truth is, raising children is just part of the Circle of Life. I've often heard people say this world is too scary to bring a child into. This is totally understandable. My feelings were the same so many decades ago. But we need to understand hormones and the "prime directive of the universe" will probably override the fear. The fear is pointless. Resistance, as The Borg would say, is futile.

You are born to serve The Expansion of the Great Intelligence of the Universe. Your part in it is not arbitrary. Your part is to be born and play. That is all. Some of us are naughty little children, and our indiscretions are broadcast loudly on the news nonstop. Fortunately, the vast majority of adults (97 percent or so according to usfacts.org) are not. Don't let the transgressions of the few on the six o'clock news keep you from getting the most out of your life, which may include having children. I know some of the naughty appear all-powerful, but they are not. Step back and take the view from outer space. See how beautiful your planet is. Come closer. Observe the might of our oceans and the comely seduction of our rolling hills and mountaintops. Look at your loved ones, be they parents, siblings, or others, and *feel* them. Love is the thing.

And the weather? What about the hell the weather brings? What about horrible accidents of all kinds? It's really all the same as it was for your parents, grandparents, great-grandparents, etc. They had the same lament. Life goes on. They too said, "How can I possibly bring a child into this terrible world?" The beat goes on—the drumbeat, your heartbeat, the beat of a thousand centuries. The love is the thing. It's the collective's show *and* each individual's performance creating to shape the world. The best you can do is model and teach your children how to win and attract the best of experiences to themselves. They will come into this life adventure with or without you. What you bring to your role makes all the difference. Enjoy your life, with or without a child, and remember—love is the thing. Come play with us. Be brave.

Strategy: Make a point of remembering "Source got this."

FRAME OF MIND: TOO BUSY TO PARENT

Frames of mind, like thinking you are too busy or anything that has to do with time, trip you up often because you buy into this time trap society has set for you. If you just stop and assess your values, you can rearrange your time, taking some away from low priority areas. Even when supporting your kids, you can choose between attending functions with or for them and simply hanging out with them. You get caught up in forward motion, the spinning wheel of activity you have launched, but you have not looked back to see if it has run your child over.

Your parent-child and business roles are not compartmentalized. As a business owner or employee, your success is inexorably linked to what's happening (or not) with your offspring, regardless of whether they're children or adults. Open your eyes to this.

Someone asked, I can't remember where, "Is your job the boss of you?" Your answer is probably "Hell yes!" I understand that, but you do get some time off. Divide that time into 50 percent child/children (at the very least) and 50 percent yourself. If you own your own business, "Is your business the boss of you, or are you the boss of your business?" How much time are you allowing for you and your family? Do what makes you happy as much as you possibly can.

I'm presuming here that being with your kids makes you happy. Are you overseeing your happiness, or are you letting something outside the family tell you, "You can't be in charge of your time. We'll take that. You have no time"? Time is not real in that sense. The only time-like thing that is real is "now." The now. There is no past, no future, only now. You are creating in the now what you want in your future.

Strategy: Instead of focusing on the clock and dealing with time, be "in the moment" and feel *what is happening in your family. Think long-term, big picture in* feeling *what you want for yourself and your family; then be real about the feelings actually being produced today. Do the feelings match with the big-picture goal? What really needs to be happening in this moment to produce* that *overall feeling in the big picture now and down the line when they're adults? You define all of that, your time, now. The time is always now.*

KNOW THERE ARE MIRACLES

You may feel it will take a miracle to have what I'm suggesting here. What do you think about miracles? Do you recognize their existence? Do you see childbirth, your birth, the world we live in as miraculous? You are a miracle. From there, know everything you encounter is a miracle. Can you name any others?

Miracles happen in spite of time. No progression in time is needed for a miracle to happen because the miracle already exists. Time is a human construct. The moment you express a desire, Source creates it. Source doesn't need time. That's why struggle and effort are not necessary. You only need to cease disbelief. As they say, "It's all in your head."

"There is no order of difficulty in miracles.
One is not 'harder' than or 'bigger' than another. They are
all the same. All expressions of Love are maximal."

~ A Course in Miracles

Strategy: Approach your meditation sessions knowing you are in focused communication with Source. Silence is the language. Learn to speak it. Learn to expect miracles.

STRATEGIES FOR LEADING THE PARENT EXAMPLE LONGTERM

1.) Address and eliminate your fears, anxieties, and phobias as prescribed in Chapter 4: Shedding Your Fears and Anxieties.

2.) Know your offspring come here with their own agendas and lessons for you to learn. Cease the urge to judge and direct *everything* they do. You'll only stress yourself out and create health problems for yourself and them.

3.) Your role is to set the example and protect, mostly get out of their way, and give yourself a break. Source is in charge of their lives as well as yours. Direct your loving directives accordingly.

Can you feel the simplified strategy I'm promoting here?

SUMMARY

Leading a family is an approximate science. Being a parent is a long-haul operation of example setting. Enjoying and appreciating each moment as you go is the best way to get the results you're seeking for you and your family. Endeavor to strike a balance in what you expect from your family. Give yourself a break. Respect the variables of what you feel and have gone through, and consider the many variables of each child and family member. Relax in this. Doing this will help offset or lessen stress and chronic disease for you and your family.

EXERCISE

1.) What is your "time frame of mind"?

____

____

____

____

____

2.) What is an example of a childhood pain you are repeating with your child or children?

____

____

____

____

____

3.) To what extent have you owned up to your deep-seated hatred of your parent(s)?

____

____

____

____

____

____

____

4.) What is your strategy for enjoying and appreciating each moment as you go along?

____

____

____

____

____

____

____

Chapter 9

EXAMINING YOUR CORE VALUES AND INTEGRITY

"Once you really *know who you are, all of your decisions will become easier. You are no longer fearfully reacting to a problem, worried about what others think, or desperately searching for an answer outside of you. Instead, you'll simply be responding to challenges with your own innate values."*

~ Dr. Mark Schillinger

In the last chapter, we looked at parents' leadership strategies. In this chapter, we explore your core values, which are the motivations behind discipline and respect.

What are your core values? Integrity? Honesty? Reliability? Commitment? Spirituality? Appreciation? What? List them, list examples of them, and list the consequences of not living by them. Then it will be easier to teach and set examples for your children. Do you stick to your core values with integrity?

Instill them into your child before they turn eighteen and magically "know it all." Remember yourself at eighteen? Looking at key insights from what you remember about your eighteen-year-old thoughts will help you get on the good foot with this.

I distinctly remember my eighteen-year-old self. I truly felt I knew it all. When I was eighteen, I felt I'd learned all I needed to know. My mother's strictness was more than I could bear. I wanted out. In college, I found a way to escape. As a member of the Black Power organization on campus, I could get housing paid for with grants to the organization. I plotted my move and left while my mother and stepfather were at work and my brother and sister were at school. This started a "pattern of abandonment," something I now realize is a result of my father having abandoned my mother and me when I was in her womb. I went on to abandon more than a few relationships when things weren't going my way. Anyway, my newfound freedom lasted only a few weeks because my mother petitioned and (no doubt) threatened the school administrators and organization leaders to have me returned. Lesson: To be truly free one must be able to independently maintain freedom.

Here are a few random things I did not know when I was eighteen:

- How money works—there is a world class caste mentality and entitlement system dictated by how much money one can squeeze out of those who labor in the first layers of the system.

- Men are very different from women.
- The degree to which racism negatively affects my life.
- The depth of the body's intricate connection to the mind and Spirit.

The truth is that life experience matters a lot. In conversations with a child who wants to run away, gentle (and not-so-gentle) reminders of how life experience matters help temper the urge to escape. Will you worry? Of course, you will. When you discover they are missing and realize they have run away, immediately seek comfort in Source. Know their own connection to Source will direct the outcome, and prepare yourself to accept whatever outcome that is.

"Get IN to your feelings, the worldly systems are a mind-programming lie. Stop attracting what you DO NOT WANT for abundant life and unlimitation!"

~ Dr. Tracey Bond

Core values grow out of the need to survive and thrive in society in a loving, efficient, and prosperous way. Values can be good or bad, bad usually leading to some form of unhappiness (injury, prison, death). For example, in the capitalist system (and others), greed flourishes as a core value and feels good to the greedy because they have no real love for others nor concern for the black mold that greed causes to grow on their souls. Their training about the consequences of theft at home was seriously lacking. The lives of the others they steal from, their siblings all, mean very little to them. Source will excavate and disinfect their souls publicly or privately.

INTEGRITY

"One of the truest tests of integrity is its blunt refusal to be compromised."

~ Chinua Achebe

What is integrity? It's the uncompromising adherence to moral and ethical principles. It's about the truth, discipline, and core values you implant in your family and your children. You are like a mighty redwood tree. Your core values are the roots that feed the tree (you) and the fruit (your children). They are absorbed energy from The Universe that helps keep you and your family safe (if they're good).

Why is integrity important? As you move through life, you become known for the trust people have in you. Doors open when you're known for honor, honesty, and integrity. For your offspring to enjoy the benefits of trust, you instill and model what it means to have integrity. For example, if you tell them you will do something, do it.

They come to understand and trust you and, in turn, model integrity in their own behavior. Be on the lookout for opportunities to express your core values to your child(ren), get their feedback showing they understand the individual values, and discuss what you value with them in conversation purposefully and often. Doing this has a way of making it so and smoothing out the wrinkles in your day.

Your calling is at the root of your integrity—it is the quiet voice of God saying, "I trust you to be the guardian of our future. I give to you the truth of what's good for us all." You've got this. Do you trust yourself?

"Live so that when your children think of fairness, caring and integrity, they think of you."

~ H. Jackson Brown, Jr.

For instance, Candice was raised to regard theft as a grave breach of trust and one of the most dastardly things a person can do. One night, as she and her three-year-old son Michael were walking home along a long and dusty road from the grocery store, two miles away, she heard a rustling sound coming from behind her. (Michael trailed her a lot when they walked because his legs were shorter.) He was unwrapping candy he had taken at the checkout stand. You know—the displays they set up to prompt impulse buying as you wait in line to be checked out? Well, she had not bought the candy. That meant he had stolen it.

Candice took the candy and asked, "Why did you take this candy?"

"Because I wanted it," Michael replied.

"Michael," she told him, "that is stealing. We don't steal. Stealing is a sin and against the law and can get you thrown in jail." He pouted.

They were at least a half mile down the road. Candice had a decision to make—simply take the candy away and scold Michael, admonishing him to never steal again, or do the most powerful and instructive thing to drive that point home by walking him back to the store to apologize to the store manager. Which do you think she did?

"We're taking this candy right back," she told him, "and you're going to apologize to the manager for stealing."

Mind you, she was dog-tired from working all day, stressed out because she barely had the money for food, and was cursing the fact that her car had finally died. The last thing she wanted to do was make the trek back to the store lugging two bags of groceries, but there was no escaping the opportunity and power of this teaching moment. They trekked back to the store and had the cashier page the manager. Michael apologized to the manager for stealing from the store, handed the candy to him, and promised to never steal again.

This was an opportunity for Candice to express the core value of not being a thief, exercise it, and influence her son powerfully in a direction she felt was very important to his future. Did the lesson stick? Michael would be the better person to answer that question. Neither she nor society (to her knowledge) have had to reprimand (jail, imprison) him for stealing. (He is a grown man now.)

A few years later when Michael was about seven, after reprimanding him and his friends and promising she'd separate them if they didn't behave, Candice overheard him telling his friends, "And she'll do it, too!"

> *"To teach is to show. You can't teach what you don't know.*
> *You can't guide where you don't go.*
> *And you can't grow what you don't sow."*
>
> ~ Kevin Peter Hall, American Actor

Many parents think they can find an opportunity later to instill a core value or lesson with their kid because in the moment they are tired, but the nuances of the specific moment contribute to the lesson: the time of day, how tired the child is, the location, etc.

Generally, embarrassing children in front of others is not a good idea. Be age-appropriate with your tactics. At three, Michael mostly absorbed the lesson. His big ego was not fully formed yet, so embarrassment was minimal. (Big ego is mostly formed by four or so.)

Training children is expert work. You are an expert training an expert. What do you do when you encounter outrageous behavior in your child? Do you overreact, punish, remain calm, become embarrassed, or skulk away? Remain calm. Sometimes going within to tap into your

Godhead yields the best outcomes even though it doesn't always feel that way in the face of some behavior. Please remember the behavior is there to get your attention.

Think about the integrity you instill (or not) in your family. Peace of mind and integrity direct the future. How do you instill it? How do you garner strength of character for yourself and your child? It's sobering to understand how important what you teach is. Make it easy. Enlist the golden rule in most of what you say and do. Understand you have this—quiet mind, easy flow. Once you maintain a conscious connection to Source, all will flow more easily: what to do, when to do it, and why you do it.

Rev. Michael Beckwith said:

> *As you begin to study the wisdom teachings…and be about the truth, the fruition is the realization of integrity. Integrity is about being integrated with the spiritual values of the Universe and also about being happy because happiness and joy mean that you're coming into integrity with your soul.*

What if you don't engage in a deeper relationship with integrity? Look around you. I distinctly remember and still see parents who have dropped the ball and let their children run them. When was the last time you saw the fruit of trees dictate to the trunk? Without integrity, challenges can sway them to the dark side. They can be broken in spirit, dishonor themselves, and lose self-respect. You are the hero in your home. Heroes thrive on integrity.

PRESSURE ON YOUR TWEEN TO BE SEXY

Pressure on your tween and teen to be sexy comes from their peers, the news, movies, all kinds of entertainment, and the media. Advertisers target them to buy and wear sexy clothing among other things. It is worrisome that our children are being targeted and sexualized at such young ages.

It's the parents' responsibility to monitor what the child is buying. I understand peer pressure is huge in your child's teens, but these years, in particular, are ripe with opportunities for parents to resist being bullied themselves (by their own kids) and to teach their kids by their example what it means to develop character, integrity, and self-respect in the face of this kind of pressure. Having them learn to recognize and ignore peer pressure and certain products in advertising helps them to become strong as adults; then they'll need to do the same for so many other products and options. We're bombarded with advertisements. It's media mind training of the worst sort. The dumbing down of America and our children can be found in many places; one is in the constant onslaught of sexual images, oversexualized pop stars, and the media. Too much of our energy and intelligence is focused on superficial rather than important things. How do you help your children take the reins of what they internalize?

When you speak to your child from the beginning of their cognitive formation in a way that respects their intelligence, they will respect your intelligence. Your child comes here with the ability to acquire and apply knowledge. They need help with the language. Their trust in you allows you to influence a lot of what they think and feel. You can tell them what leads to what (age appropriately) and describe the connection to negative outcomes. Then ask them what they think. Talk *with* them, not *at* them.

Sexy products are connected to premature sexual activity. Let's stand against this kind of pandering to our kids that fattens someone else's wallet. If you don't buy it, the companies will cease this nonsense. Sex, though important, appeals to our lowest instincts. Raising a teenager includes helping them learn to harness and redirect sexual energy into academic excellence, sports, and other worthy pursuits. They will have plenty of time later for carnal knowledge and the issues that come with it.

Have you made a list of your core values, and are you instilling them in your children with integrity? Are your core values more salient to you now? Do you model them with integrity for your offspring?

SUMMARY

Step up with integrity and integrate your core values. Examine your priorities and find out what you really want for yourself and your family. If you co-parent, the two of you must meet privately and come up with the core values you will instill with integrity, meaning you will demonstrate them through your example.

EXERCISE

1.) Do you remember yourself at eighteen? Write some key insights from what you remember about your eighteen-year-old thoughts. What do you remember most?

____

____

____

____

____

____

2.) Knowing where your child is at all times (to the best of your ability) is a tall order. What are some consequences of not knowing?

____

____

____

____

____

____

____

3.) Are you a role model of compassion who shows your child the benefits of a loving attitude? How consistent are you at this?

____

____

____

____

____

4.) How do you go about helping your child harness and redirect sexual energy into academic excellence, sports, and other worthy pursuits?

____

____

____

____

____

Chapter 10

BEING HEARD

"At any given time, there are three things going on inside of us: 1) the laws we believe about ourselves, 2) how we behave in response to those laws, and 3) what we believe about the world. On top of that are the rules that govern the world we see."

~ Garrett J. White

In the previous chapter, we addressed core values and integrity. In this chapter, we will talk about being heard.

Note that Garrett White's quote above applies to each of your individual children and you, your co-parent, and other members of the world. Children are picking up "laws" about themselves from their parents as they go along, especially during their first five years. They behave in response to those laws.

Does your child listen to you? Oh, they hear you. They just don't care about what you have to say. They have their own focus and agendas.

PARENT PARADISE

How do you overcome distractions and help your children understand what you're saying? Many distractions invade their days—noise in the household and noise in their heads included. To avoid having to say the same things over and over again, consider helping to get rid of distractions. If that isn't enough, change what you're saying and/or ask them to repeat what you've said and explain why you've said it. (This is where having conversations comes in.) I know it feels like a lot of work in the moment, but it will help your child to listen to and understand you.

What is your unique perspective, your "unique value proposition" (UVP)? We all come from one place. We each emerge from Source with our unique perspective, to enjoy our unique existence. Our parent perspective always needs to consider and be mindful of the offspring perspective. You were once a child yourself.

"When you parent, it's crucial you realize you aren't raising a 'mini-me,' but a spirit throbbing with its own signature. For this reason, it's important to separate who you are from who each of your children is."

~ Dr. Shefali Tsabary

As you go within to uncover more of your mystery, light begins to pour in on this being a parent situation, and you can clearly navigate the steps taking you from parent hell to parent paradise. Here are a few things to recognize along the way:

1.) Your pain is a choice. You are choosing pain when you ignore its solution. Your meditation and fear-elimination practice can alleviate all sorts of pain.
2.) You may not be allowing prosperity. Finances cause a lot of stressful yelling and negative reactions to what kids are doing. Use meditation to help *allow* your wealth and prosperity to flow in. Your engagement in meditation helps you remember who you are and helps the rushing energy of prosperity, stress relief, mental clarity, emotional stability, and joy to flow to you.
3.) Maintaining balance in communication feels good, gets respect, gives respect, and sounds like the calm whispers of the wind, the soft purr of a jaguar engine, or the crack of thunder in a storm—depending on what is needed in the moment to restore balance. Leaning too far in either direction brings up a not-so-good feeling. That not-so-good feeling is your cue to get balanced.

ADULTS PERPETUATE THEIR CHILDHOOD PAIN

Myth: Repetition creates change. Truth: Right repetition creates change.

Using the same verbal disciplinary content repetitively is boring and tedious—to adults. Children can obviously hear you say something over and over and over again because their free spirits and open minds give wing to the noise you're making. Initially, nothing is in place in their mind to keep your voice commands…er…requests from going in one ear and out the other. Save your breath for saying the warm, loving things your family longs to hear. You quite literally need to save your breath on at least a couple of levels: environmentally and in your relationships. Use clear, loving communication in relationships and in dealing with children. Repeating commands over and over again is a stressful activity that has been passed on from generation to generation. Right repetition creates change; not nagging, loud, or aggressive repetition.

I was walking around feeling bad and accepting that feeling for much of my life. I came to think of it as normal. At various times, the feelings of fear and anxiety were so strong I could hardly concentrate. Whatever the strength or intensity, these feelings are bad news. Even the very subtle ones have a devastating influence on your long-term health because they can compound over time and snowball into chronic diseases. Health problems aren't entirely caused by aging or various other obvious causes, such as genetics and injury. How you feel is central to what you attract in all aspects of your life: your relationships, health, and wealth. You inherently know stress is not good for you and not normal. Clearly and consciously understand it's not normal to carry stress around. The moment you feel the tightening of stress in your neck, shoulders, head, or wherever, loosen it. Use whichever relaxing technique is convenient in the moment.

Are you a slave to emotions and negative feelings from your childhood? You received these emotions and feelings from your parents, and they got them from their parents, and so on. Would you be surprised to find your offspring have the same complaints about you that you have with your parents? How about complaints about the way you handled things in the opposite way your parents did to avoid doing what your parents did? These feelings flower in the ever-present, constant family confusion that serves to compound chaos and stress. It's killing you softly and sometimes, not so softly. Just because you can ingest slow poison, doesn't mean you should.

Do you find you lash out automatically at your family, coworkers, or strangers? Do you feel sad, low, or dejected most of the time? Are you easily angered, irritated, or vexed?

Stop in the moment (and in random moments throughout the day):

1.) To monitor your thoughts or whether you feel you're about to be angry. This could be anger at a person, situation, or some other trigger.

2.) Assess what you're feeling.

3.) Implement the appropriate healthy action—whether you're dealing with a difficult adult or child, stop in the moment, assess, and take appropriate action. Do you need a meditation break? Deep breathing? Progressive muscle relaxing? Yoga? A walk in the park?

Capture "silence of mind" and have it extend throughout your day(s). That is where the magic is.

"There are only two ways to live your life.
One is as though nothing is a miracle.
The other is as though everything is a miracle."

~ Albert Einstein

Make it a point to see the beauty in everything, even your misbehaving kid. Most of life is beautiful. You just need to change your perspective and see it. Meditation will help you change your perspective and come to have and appreciate the active moment-to-moment awareness of peace.

IS YOUR CHILD ABUSING YOU?

Is your child abusing you? Stay in touch with your "alpha-ness"! The foundation of "how it is, is what *you* say it is." As the parent, remember you got here first, and you created this monster. Don't let your child be the boss.

This reminds me of a scene I witnessed in the mall while Christmas shopping. I was sitting in the rest area around the tree with parents watching children play when I saw a woman walking by carrying two bags. Her whining, tired son was begging her, no, insisting, she pick him up and carry him. Mind you, he was only a head shorter than his mother. Just as I thought she was going to turn around and give him what for (I was tired of hearing him too), do you know what she did?

She picked him up and carried him and the bags as far as I could see, probably all the way to the car. Astonishing!

I knew in that moment parents needed me to come out of retirement to help them temper their obnoxious, cute bioidenticals. I see way too many parents disrespected or bullied by their children. This may be the result of doing the opposite of what their parents did. Perhaps their parents were too strict or abusive bullies. It's understandable to want to do better than your parents did, but sometimes we overcompensate. This is harmful to the child. If your child bullies you, they'll bully others. As they grow, they become even more unmanageable. When they get out into the world as adults, their relationships suffer. The qualities of those attracted to them may be unhealthy or dangerous. Remember, you are protecting their futures also. Prisons are full of bullies (and people who were tired of being bullied). Their work life will be affected. At work, you build working relationships with people. You want to attract good people. Promotions and success depend on it.

Many parents feel that if they're too strict, they will border on being hypocrites and their children will find them out and disrespect them even more. But it's really easier than that. If they just realize disciplining with integrity, for example, helps keep their child safe and provides a strong foundation that helps build character, they could relax and be more confident in what they're doing.

Balance and context are key. *How* you say *how it is* makes all the difference. What came before and what comes after you say how it is determines whether a satisfactory upbringing is underway. Respect is earned, even by parents, and I assure you letting your child run you shows a serious lack of respect from both the child and you. Regardless of how cute our babies are, it's in their best interest and society's that parents take charge. Don't let your child abuse you!

If you are dealing with chaos, remember, chaos is the thing that polishes your patience and creates the golden memories that keep you warm in old age. Your children want nothing more than your loving, full attention, which is best given when you're 100 percent in the moment with them. In those 100 percent moments, don't forget you are the alpha.

TUNE INTO INTUITION

"Intuition is important and is not respected these days. People stress themselves needlessly because they're not listening to their intuition."

~ Dr. Yasemin Gokalp

It's a wonderful Fall Festival/Halloween day. You're sitting outside in a meadow in an audience of parents watching a Halloween play in which your child is performing. The air is crisp and refreshing. The sun is gentle on your face.

The play is going well. Everyone is beaming with pride as their progeny do their thing when you notice a metal beam is slowly giving way over your child's head! You rise to rush to stop the performance and clear the stage, but there isn't time!

In your mind, you shout for your child to step back! At that moment, your child steps back just as the beam falls in front of them. Coincidence? I think not.

Telepathy? Intuition? Spirituality.... Is your parenting sense disabled? Your aura or radiance has an effect via "silent transmission." What are you giving off to your children? Intuition is the ability to understand something immediately, without the need for conscious reasoning. Telepathy is the communication of thoughts or ideas by means other than the known senses...it's via Source.

Whether your child is five or fifty, your connection with them is facilitated and integrated with telepathy and intuition. They are a means of making parenting easier but are often ignored in that regard. You are connected to your offspring on heavenly levels. A lot of what you communicate is not in words—a lot is telepathy and vibration. We have some level of these connections with everyone.

By this same token, you don't realize how deeply your stress affects your child(ren). My misery as a divorced mother stemmed from a lack of understanding of the depth of the connection I had with my child. The result was needless suffering due to poor communication.

When my son was in my womb, I talked with him all the time, as I'm sure you did with your offspring. Once he was born and right on through age twelve or so, we had a strong non-verbal connection. (Then hormones hit.) I miss those times. In a happier time with my ex-husband, at about 2:30 p.m. one day, as I was descending the stairs from the second floor of a prospective real estate client's home, I felt a strong jolt in my chest that almost dropped me to my knees. It was at this precise moment that my then husband had fallen three stories to the ground at his job on a construction site many miles away!

This was an instantaneous telepathic intuitive communication on our part. To me, at that time in our relationship, it meant something like we were truly bonded. Imagine my devastation and heartbreak at finding it wasn't enough to keep us together.

Then there is the other evidence: evidence of ESP between twins and other multiple birth siblings cannot be denied. More than enough evidence of our special connections has existed through millennia. Let's not debate gravity. I say all that to say this:

Many parents think if they do things harder (like work harder or press their child to do what they, the parent, want them to do), they will get what they want, but it's really easier than that. If they would only realize that they have built-in psychological and spiritual powers, then they would give themselves a break, reduce their stress, and open themselves to the growth and discovery of a far more interesting and fulfilling life and happier kids.

Elizabeth Lloyd Mayer, a converted skeptic and author of *Extraordinary Knowing: Science, Skepticism, and the Inexplicable Powers of the Human Mind*, reports:

> As I probed, patients, colleagues, and even a famed neurosurgeon confessed, often with embarrassment, that sometimes they just knew things—the exact moment to operate, the hidden location of a deadly disease. Their shame intrigued me and confirmed my sense that our reliance as a culture on conclusions based on readily identifiable evidence forces us to tiptoe around experiences we can't explain instead of facing our deep-seated fear of the unknown.

Helpful with all kids, which includes kids with special needs, telepathy comes from the idea all beings originate from the same Source. Many examples exist of intuition at work. You probably have many you recognize yourself. Intuition has been known to save many lives. I put such phenomena on par with seeing gravity or the discovery of the Higgs boson subatomic particle, aka "the God particle." Endless experiments are done in these arenas, and the assumptions are eventually proven true. Until then, you can happily go about your way expanding your faculties and using what "is." Science proves nature. Nature got here first. Science is catching up.

Also, significant evidence all over shows that hypnosis (the power of suggestion) works for weight loss, smoking cessation, addiction control, pain reduction, and now even child discipline issues. How would your life go if you regularly tapped into your intuition? Do you tap into it?

Are you teaching your offspring to tap into theirs?

Our Source communicates with us through our intuition. The word intuition comes from the mid-fifteenth-century word *intuicioun*, "insight, direct or immediate cognition, spiritual perception."

My recommendations for beginning to bridge the gap with our intuition are:

1.) Pay more attention to adding joy to the moments in your day.
2.) Relax more. Stress never or way less.
3.) Listen to the thoughts and feelings you have inside that feel good and amplify them.

Can you take ownership of helping your children hear you?

SUMMARY

Your child doesn't necessarily have to always listen to you. You have to listen to yourself and to them. If you're nagging, less is more. Work to deepen your ordinary knowledge of them. Use your intuition more.

EXERCISE

1.) Where do you think the line is between responsible parenting and child abuse?

____

____

____

____

2.) Please write about a time you strongly recognized your intuition.

____

____

____

____

3.) Does your child or adult offspring listen to you? Why or why not?

____

____

____

____

Chapter 11

TALKING IN A WAY YOUR CHILD WILL LISTEN

"Children have never been very good at listening to their elders but they have never failed to imitate them."

~ James Baldwin

In the previous chapter, we addressed helping your child listen to you. In this chapter, we will look at how to talk to your child so they listen.

Baldwin's point in the quote above is the very essence of what's going on with parent/child communications. How would you have liked to have been spoken to when you were a child, or at any age? Do you speak to your parents the way they spoke to you? Do you want your child to speak to you the way you speak to them?

TALK LINE: WE ARE NOT FRIENDS

By talk line, I mean the place in communicating with your child where you draw the line at being disrespected. I witnessed a back-and-forth between a mother and child recently that made the hair on my neck stand up.

She was attempting to protect him from danger (he had to be seven or eight) as he was flying downhill on a blade scooter. As she called his name, he ignored her or, on every other call, barked back, "What!" instead of stopping or slowing down. Cliffs, trees, and rocks were waiting to enforce discipline where she failed. Now, the old me (who happens to still live inside me) wanted to snatch that little dude by the arm and hold him until the proper authority could round the corner and address the situation, but I didn't. I didn't know if she would have appreciated my help. Times have changed. I knew it was none of my business, but I remember in my own childhood, when a village mother would do just that until the child's mother could round the corner, catch up, and take over. But I digress. I kept walking.

My point here is that sooner or later when trying to talk with your children, it is almost certain they will verbally or behaviorally disrespect you. In that precise moment of disrespect, you must drop everything and address it. In other words, your tone and the subject changes. In the above instance, after his first "what," my answer, in tone and texture, would have been "Who do you think you're talking to?" Based on our history and his recognition of my tone, he would have stopped in his tracks and waited or slowed down as requested.

I could go on about this, but suffice it to say, if he lost control and ran into a tree, it would have ruined a very pleasant sunny afternoon and likely he and his mother would have ended up in the emergency room. It's most effective to explain to children in the *precise* moment they are *never* allowed to speak to you that way, and you are *not* one of their friends but the person responsible for them. Reintroduce yourself. Tell them, "You are my deepest love, and I am your protector, your parent, the one who has come before you and staked out danger. I demand your respect at all times." (You may need to continue.) "At some point, if you listen and learn the lessons I teach you now, you will become an adult. At that point, you will have gained the wisdom to give back to your younger brothers, sisters, and your children, but for now, appreciate me and what I teach you as I appreciate you and what you teach me. Let's respect each other. Don't talk back to me." You get my drift? What would you add to this talk line?

COMMUNICATION CYCLE OF THE PARENT-CHILD DYNAMIC

"It's no surprise we fail to tune into our children's essence. How can we listen to them, when so many of us barely listen to ourselves? How can we feel their spirit and hear the beat of their heart if we can't do this in our own life?"

~ Dr. Shefali Tsabary, Author of *A Radical Awakening*

Does how you communicate with your child promote positive growth? The parent's perspective must always consider and appreciate the child's perspective. Parents often expect the parent-child communication cycle dynamic to be simple. The idea is simple, but there is more to it.

Here is the cycle:

Parent message > Child interprets message > Child critiques message (in their mind) (depends on age) > Child acts on message (or not) > Parent message.

This is a simplistic view. You need to make allowances for unknown variables to keep your cool about how the "child acts on message (or not)." Here are some things to consider for each communication/message/lesson:

What kind of noise is in your head when you are formulating your message/lesson/edict?

This is a big one because we often act without thinking. Often, we need to just stop and take five seconds to see how we feel. Think and then proceed with a message based on some intelligent thought rather than a negative emotion. If your emotion is too negative, you should table the lesson until you calm down. Then write it out and review it before delivery.

What mental state is your child in when you deliver your message?

"Don't raise your voice. When kids are scared, they go into fight-or-flight, learning centers of the brain shut down. Your child can't learn when you yell. It's always more effective to intervene calmly and compassionately. Yelling loses credibility with your child. Kids become less open to your influence."

~ Dr. Laura Markham

Can they truly "hear" us, or are they in pain, physically or emotionally? Some pain they've caused themselves works well with our message to help them. If they are in too much pain or too distracted to pay attention, they can't hear us. In this case, just wait.

Write out what you want to say and schedule a time to talk with them when you have their full attention. A good time is right before you give them something they want.

Do you use visual aids, stories, or threats to help get your point across? Threats and fearmongering are weak, give weak incentive for learning, and feed negative noise in their heads. Better to be creative when communicating with children. It's more fun when we put our mind and creative juices into talking with our children. This requires more time and intellect on your part, but on the bright side, it expresses more love for them and helps ward off Alzheimer's for you!

Will the child understand what you mean, or is it open to interpretation from their perspective? Again, this requires thought. Cover this base. It makes all the difference in the world, especially with teenagers. How would you have interpreted the message when you were that age? Really think and be honest about the answer. Put yourself in the child's shoes—how many meanings could be in play? Sometimes the result requires a longer conversation (communication cycle). The following cycle is dynamic as well:

Child message > Parent interprets message > Parent critiques message (in their mind) > Parent acts on message...and repeat.

How much true listening to your child do you do? This back-and-forth energy-dynamic is to be respected, cherished, and ultimately enjoyed.

PULL IN YOUR MOJO

You're rushing down the street, excited and anxious to get to your business appointment on time. You glance at your watch. It looks like you'll just make it...when...you realize...you left your baby on the bus!

Is your mojo out of whack? If you find yourself running ragged and letting things drop through the cracks, it's a sign your mojo is out of whack. Get yourself together.

What is your mojo? It's your "Universal Resource," the universal joint in the drive shaft that is your life. It's your magic, the spark that gets things done.

We often forget the power that moves our lives comes from within. Some of us don't know it's there. We need it for raising children. If it's scattered, pull it in.

What do I mean by scattered mojo? Mojo gets scattered when we attempt to focus on more than one thing at a time. Our energy gets scattered in all directions like a single beam of light going through a prism. Remember prisms? The light goes through one side and gets divided into many weaker beams than the light as a single, focused point. The resulting light is watered down, weaker, and fainter. That's why multitasking isn't a good idea. The brain can do only one thing at a time, and it actually does that—just one thing at a time even though we think we're doing many.

What does all this have to do with communicating with children? Well, scattered mojo—watered down by too many things to do—is a leading cause of grief, pain, and depression. It's an absolute self-fulfilling prophecy—a wet, soggy mess that needs airing out and fluffing up. If you're impatient or snappy with your family, check your feelings. If you are overwhelmed, it's a sign your mojo is out of whack. The task at hand (raising the child) is an all-consuming love challenge, the ultimate life project, second to none. Requirements are that you ambitiously seek to create the best family unit you can. To do that, you must have your energy for family intact and do your best to refresh it daily. My favorite activities for refreshing it are meditation and relaxation. What do you do to refresh your energy daily?

As the dean and chancellor of Home University and your wee ones' superhero, it's imperative to keep in touch and in tune with your mojo. Parenthood is a serious eighteen-year project. You pick up the mantle and engage as a life coach when they are born. You are training your children for greatness as you're being trained in grace. Once the child is here, what is the big benefit to you? The benefit, if you allow it, is you are forever changed and inspired to be better and the best you could possibly be. Children are your call to Mt. Olympus. Isn't that what deep, unconditional love does?

Why is mojo important when communicating with our children? Well, aside from what I've already said, children under five are still in tune with "Original Mojo." It's the part of communication that's there before intuition and telepathy. It colors and flavors the message being communicated. As dean and chancellor of Home University, does your curriculum account for your children's outrageous genius? Does it respect and reflect yours?

I won't dissect the intimate components of mojo here. The good news is, you can relax and just let it show and express itself. Remember this: Your exercise is to "relax":

Rest.
Enter peace.
Loosen your joints, muscles, and nerves.
Allow Source to induce…
Xquisite Silence, noiseless mind.

Mojo injects play. Let me tell you about one of my favorite uncles. His nickname was Jabbo. He's long gone now, but his spirit, his mojo, lives on in me. Like most people, he had a dark side, but for me, it was his mojo that stood out. He was upbeat and funny and was always playing and wrestling with us kids. I was born and raised poor in the South. My whole extended family was poor, including my uncle, but he exuded a magical loud, jovial confidence. I think the other expression for it is *joie de vivre*, joy of life. Toward the end of his life, his dastardly deeds caught up with him, but his big contribution to my life was the joy he brought me every time I saw him—having a boring afternoon? Wrestle with Uncle Jabbo. He was always down with it for us kids. Stranded at school in the rain? He'd swoop in and pick us up. He always seemed to magically be there to rescue us. (I'm sure my mother called on him for help.)

Uncle Jabbo illustrates the influence and contribution of others as well as parents.

When things are going your way and in a consistent flow, your mojo is working. When you're able to identify it and work with it until it's virtually tangible, you can help your kids identify it in themselves. Is this a subject of study and exploration in your home curriculum? When your kids get a handle on their mojo, they're happier and more things go their way (that you want them to have go their way). Heaven forbid the kids have more mojo than you. What do you think would happen in that case? Would you be at their mercy? Would they bully you?

Honing a skill like harnessing their mojo when they're children helps make their adult life a lot happier and easier. You've probably met people you considered magical—whatever they touched turned to gold. Well, you've read about them at least....

It doesn't have to be only the upper tenth of a percent we recognize as having working mojo. Some truly spectacular teachers, scientists, and Lyft drivers are out there who have it together as well. What is your measurement of success? Is it happiness? How does one develop the expression of their mojo? Remember this: Your innate essence powers your mojo. To develop an ever-flowing stream of mojo, joy, and things going your way, all it takes is quieting your negative thoughts and negative feelings absolutely. Developing that *absoluteness* is the exercise.

What if you don't care about getting your mojo working? The wheels come off the tricycle and you fall off. Have you ever heard the expression, "One cannot live on bread alone"? You need humor, flavor, and variety to be happy and healthy. Your central nervous system sparks off of a sprinkle of sugar—the sweetness in your life.

Your children are doomed to boring themselves and everyone else to death with their crassness if you don't show them mojo is something to aspire to. Join them in putting the electronics down and hanging out with their electrical insides. From a global standpoint, a substantial dose of humor flavored with humanity, understanding, and compassion would cure a lot of ills, particularly in people who want to go to war. Using that power for good—good meaning loving people—is what mojo is all about.

Nationally, as parents, we lead the way in setting love, joy, and understanding [aka mojo] as the priority in how we conduct ourselves among ourselves and other nations. Our vested interest in our children's future happiness and well-being and our own is the motivating factor. We sentence ourselves to self-annihilation or implosion if we fail.

What is your choice in this matter? It all starts locally and in the home. The attitudes, attributes, integrity, humanity, respect, compassion, and joy all take root in the home, your domain. If it is to be, it's up to you. Are you on board with this? How easy is this? It's as easy as letting it be. It's as easy as sunshine. It's as easy as you already know it all. When you, as a babe, dawned upon this planet, you came here with a purity of spirit. Remember this: Your pure spirit is your *joie de vivre*, your mojo. It is the seat of your mojo. May it reign forever.

Your children come here with this same purity of spirit. When you remember that, identify it in yourself at the same time. One beauty of having children is they remind you of who you really are. So, tell me, what is your favorite way to keep your mojo workin'?

Strategy: To get your Mojo workin': meditate, listen to music, dance, sing, and engage in creative activities you enjoy like painting, creating, building/making stuff, etc. Do some of these things with your loved ones.

WHO IS SPEAKING?

Speak to your child (and other people) from your godhead. Your godhead is the part of your brain, heart, and spirit that is Source. That part of you that is "in Joy" at all times and is compassionate, loving, and patient. Speak from there and give your wisdom to your offspring through your personal story, your feelings, and experiences. They matter! (Have you written your story?)

Concrete steps toward having your children learn how to think through the consequences of their choices—in what to eat, drink, say, and do—begin with teaching them to ask the right questions of themselves (and possibly others) before they act. Questions like: Is there a chance doing this will make me sick or kill me? Is it wise to trust this (person, thing, situation)? What could the consequences now or in the future be if I do this?

What are some of your best questions? Can you put an emergency stop button on all the negative feedback you give your children? Okay, how about most of it? If you can't, make a point of saying and meaning five or more positive things for every one negative thing you say. As you know, minds cling to the negative. This ratio of positive feedback is to offset growing negative self-esteem. Take opportunities to praise your child(ren) daily. It builds their confidence and offsets negativity.

Does your child/teen know you experienced bullying as a child/teen (if you did)? Knowing this helps them through their challenges. Talk with them about your experiences and the experiences of others. Do not weigh your child down with the yawning weight of your adult insecurity, though. Find adult friends to confide in. Maintain your alpha-ness. Look into your child's feelings—not an idle surface look. Don't do a drive-by. Don't phone it in. Engage your magnificent brain and deep well of compassion. Can you slow down long enough to do this?

ATTITUDE

"Life is 10 percent what happens to you
and 90 percent how you react
to what happens to you."

~ Chuck Swindoll

Ensure your children have a clear understanding of what attitude is.

Did you understand what attitude was when you were eighteen to twenty-two years old? The boss at my first job when I was eighteen would refer to my "poor attitude," but I had no clue what that was. Do your children understand what attitude is, positive or negative?

The definition of attitude here is: a settled way of thinking or feeling about someone or something, typically one that is reflected in a person's behavior, positive or negative.

Explain that their attitude, positive or negative, will affect their success in getting what they want now and in the future. Looking for good attitudes? Teach your children and teens *now* that *how* they meet disappointment influences how happy they are. When you meet disappointment, leave it (the feeling) immediately. It is not worth your energy and will only drag you down.

Do you understand better now how to talk to your child so they will listen?

SUMMARY

The parenting perspective always needs to be mindful of the offspring perspective. A lot of talking needs to be done, not yelling. Just incorporate paying attention to what you're saying as part of the fun of being a parent.

EXERCISE

1.) What are your insights into the parent-child communication cycle?

____

____

____

____

____

2.) What negative communication do you often give your child?

____

____

____

____

____

3.) Write four or more positive communications you can give your child to offset the above negative communication.

____

____

____

____

4.) Relationship issues are rooted in the soil of the parent-child dynamic. What kind of relationships are your children bound to have based on this fact?

____

____

____

____

Chapter 12

UNDERSTANDING WHAT YOU ARE COMMUNICATING

"That we are surrounded by deep mysteries is known to all but the incurably ignorant."

~ Chinua Achebe

In the last chapter, we looked at talking to your child in a way that will help them listen. In this chapter, we focus on understanding what you are communicating.

When you speak, do you think it's random, logical noise you're making to get a point across?

Chinua Achebe's quote above (for my purposes here) addresses the intuition, telepathy, and six-plus senses in play in our day-to-day communications. It helps explain why calm energy influences and brings on calm energy. Why are you emotional when you see someone being emotional?

We are so complex.

Protecting and nurturing to the best of your ability in an easy way is all that is necessary. However, your ability to protect requires a degree of cooperation from your child as they get older. Understanding the kinds of communication between you and your child is key to getting their cooperation.

What are your unreasonable expectations of your child's thought processes? For example, you give a command, "Go clean up your room." The child doesn't do it. You become annoyed. Expectations that cause annoyance stress you *and* them. Feel free to cease and desist. (Your child thinks the room is clean enough. You needed to be specific. "Pick your clothes up off the floor in your room, etc.")

Mirrors of love surround us in the faces of our children. Do you see what you want to see? Look with more than your eyes. Children are made smarter with meditation (communing with Source) and conversation. Are you asking questions rather than giving simple commands? The way you hear something is colored by your psyche, as it is for them. The way you hear something from your offspring may not be the way they meant it (and vice versa). To what extent do you monitor your reactions before you act on them? Promoting emotional intelligence in the child *and* parent is a by-product of compassionate communication with your child(ren).

CHILD ABANDONMENT

I'm using the term child abandonment in a broader, less obvious sense here. What I mean is, in many cases, the woman becomes pregnant, and the man disappears. To me, the child the woman is carrying *and* the woman have been abandoned. This is the story for many, many people. It's my story as well.

My dear mother, being the naïve sixteen-year-old most girls are, fell in love with the handsome young man who managed to get into her panties. Raging hormones did their part, as did the old-fashioned expectation girls had in those days that sex must lead to marriage. Sex did not lead to marriage—it led to my mother's pregnancy with me. He got another girl pregnant six months later. My sister (whom I wouldn't know existed for fourteen years) and I were born six months apart. (Who knows if there were others?) He married the other girl, abandoned my heartbroken mother and me, and then moved to another state.

Three years later, my mother married my stepfather, who gave me his name, and for a long time, I was perfectly fine. A few years later, my mother and stepfather were separated. One day, my stepfather came by to pick up my brother and me for visitation fun as he had been doing every week for a while (I don't remember how long), but that day, he left me behind.

Crying and hiccupping, I asked my mother, "Why can't I go?"

"Because he is not your father," my mother said.

"Who is my father?" I asked.

My mother silently walked away.

For me, this emotional neglect (and other abuse) led to an ingrained lack of self-esteem and a very deep lack of self-worth. I became a guided missile looking for affection from *anyone*. It led to my continuously reaching and grasping for attention. A child or young adult can easily become a victim because predators of all shades look for needy people. This book and my practice will help you alleviate these issues using the insights I've gained in my seventy-four-plus years.

Then there's the other kind of abandonment—the kind where the parent is there physically, but they mostly ignore the child, don't listen, or often shut the child down when the child is trying to communicate with them. That's abandonment also. It's not a good feeling. My mother was half-guilty of this, but you see, she too had been abandoned by her father and then by my father. I dare say my grandmother had the same experience. As you see, this buck had to stop somewhere. It stopped with me.

Child neglect is child abuse!

To raise happy, healthy, well-adjusted children who become happy, healthy, and well-adjusted adults, we need to listen and stimulate, nurture and protect. Neglect and/or bullying are abuse and damage the child and the adult they will become. Aggressive abuse sounds and feels like a lot of noise, screaming, in-your-face confrontations, and sometimes, physical pain. Neglect is quiet, overlooks the nurturing discipline needed in any given instance, and feels numb.

Focus and negotiation build and enhance your loving family synergy. This book will help you with that.

Everyone wants and needs to be listened to. You validate a person's existence by giving them attention. Truly listening and participating in their lives shows them they are valuable and loved. You get far more cooperation and far less chaos when you do this. If you find you are guilty of behaving in non-loving ways toward your child, think back to your own childhood. Were you ignored? Shut down often? Did you feel alone a lot? Are you from a single-parent household or did you live that way for a long time? Did you have both parents, but they worked a lot and had little energy for you when they got home? Are you repeating a pattern of emotional abuse and neglect?

You need to be disciplined and look into yourself to change the pattern. I know you're tired. This book will help you find ways around your tiredness. Are you in your head about money or some other concern and totally distracted? Put your arms around your child and breathe with them. Whisper how much you love them in their ear and have whispered conversations with them. You'll find it relaxing. They'll find it endearing. Most of all, you'll stop the pattern of abandonment. Have you considered you may be engaged in child abandonment emotionally?

You can get caught up in day-to-day things and forget to smell the wafting fragrance of flowers and fresh-cut grass. If you take a moment, you can hear all of the sounds outside, then inside.... How many different bird sounds can you hear outside? What about insects? Inside, listen to the steady hum of electricity flowing through your home; then isolate the sound of the refrigerator, then the computer...then your heartbeat. Listen and see with your offspring. Make a game of it—and play often.

HARD DRIVE TO EASY DESTRUCTION—PARENT CRASH

What have you done to yourself? Roll that movie back and take a look....

Hard drive to easy destruction...sounds like a movie title, doesn't it? It is a movie title. It's the title of what stressed parents do daily, moment to moment in the movie that is their life, and it leads to crashing in exhaustion.

If you get some rest over the weekend, it's over by Monday morning. The "hard drive" in this metaphor is the chunk of your brain that will not let you truly relax. This constant "pressing" on your soul, mind, and spirit is draining and causes you to crash into impatience with the ones you love and yourself.

Easy destruction to yourself is the result: prematurely aging body and nerves, decreased vitality, and delayed/unrealized dreams. You owe it to yourself to remember, as you strive to nurture and educate the entire child, you need to include the child within you that did not get their full serving of the same. Your creativity is to blossom right alongside the little human you are raising. Don't neglect yourself now that you know better.

Pamela recalls when her son was a teenager he would help her out with chores around the house because she had to be at work. She was getting up early every day to get to the office and staying up late doing research, drawing up client proposals, and getting presentations together. She couldn't even keep her eyes open on Sunday movie theater outings—bobbing in and out of waking.

One of the chores her son took over was waxing the kitchen and family room floors. Tired, she'd praise him on how beautiful they were. She was so glad to have them done. He relished the praise.

At some point when she was finally rested, months and many waxes and praises later, she noticed a significant area of the floor was done terribly...she chastised him...she could hear the hurt and anguish in his voice when he replied, "You said they were beautiful, and now you're taking it back." This was a severe blow to his feelings of accomplishment and ruinous to the deep level of trust he had in her.

Had she not been so tired, she would have done a proper inspection in the beginning, re-instruction, and avoided the rift in their relationship. Working yourself into exhaustion causes this kind of callousness. This period in her life really aged her and initiated an autoimmune disease in her body. She apologized to him, but the damage was done—to them both.

Get a handle on how you're treating yourself and reverse the tide. Crash into patience and stress relief. Practice letting go. The village elders I encountered at parent meetings once told me, in the raising of my son, "Choose your battles." You don't need to be undone by every little thing or even most things. Often it's not life threatening and you can let it go—relax.

ALCOHOL AND DRUGS IN PARENTHOOD

Stress and aggravation happen when we forget who we are. Many stressed parents have symptoms resembling substance withdrawal. Alcohol facts, drug facts, and facts about depression describe a lot of what overwhelmed or lackluster parenting looks like: anxiety, restlessness, irritability, insomnia, confusion, hyper-vigilance, disorientation, and sometimes acute psychotic behavior—and that's if you are a sober parent.

Imagine how intense this situation is for the child if the parent is a moderate to heavy drinker. Now imagine the child follows this example and experiments with alcohol and drugs.

Okay. I've been accused of being too heavy. So I'll lighten it up. Hey, how about those Warriors?

Break's over. Look, I've been there. I was a depressed parent. I was drinking to drown my pain from divorce and only God knows what else. I was doing drugs of all kinds. I was overtly stupid about a whole range of things. My poor son; I hope he's okay. The reports on his well-being are excellent, by the way. Looks like I snapped out of it in time; there's hope for us all.

What I'm saying here is: Let's look at getting into "recovery" before it's too late for a good relationship with our children. If your child is still under two, you could do a complete clean-up, and they'd never know the difference. If they're older, you can monitor and improve alternately until you're in the clear.

No one said parenthood was going to be all easy. If they did, they lied. Fine jewels (great parents) are pressed from tremendous heat and pressure over time (and a lot of joy). Your lot in life is to endure varying degrees of pressure, as the diamond you are, until you get the life thing right. Your choice is to address your feelings about your difficulties the hard way or the easy way. It's up to you.

POWER TRIPS FLIP GOOD INTENTIONS

What are power trips? Power trips, in this instance, are communications with your child(ren) and family in which you seek to dominate and "win." It's having it your way no matter what anyone says.

Do power trips and struggle seem to dominate many of the exchanges you have with your child(ren)? It's a major drain on your energy. I know you wonder sometimes how you can possibly keep it up for eighteen-plus years—but you will.

In everyday life, if the parent *and* child engage in power trips, no matter what you say, it's a constant battle to make any headway. Can you see how this is exhausting? Can you feel it? Write this down: My battle is with myself. It's take on the battle or retreat. Retreat is not a real option. If you retreat, you both lose.

Getting your point across in a single battle or skirmish, no matter what it is, becomes more important than winning the war, or in this case, driving home the ultimate lesson. What is the ultimate lesson? You decide that as you go along. They are many and varied. The goal is to get your children to adulthood, happy, healthy, wise, and fulfilled.

Your battle is with yourself. It may help to look at your child and see yourself. Recall yourself at their age. This may seem abstract, but it is a worthwhile exercise. When you see yourself, compassion can kick in. Savvy can kick in. You start to remember the games you played with your parents. You gain insight into how to respond in the most effective way.

Often the most effective response is no response at all. Save your breath. Let the chips fall where they may. Think of the lesson from touching a hot stove. Let it be.

The home environment offers support. Your voice is not the only element in teaching. Your composure teaches; looking into your child's eyes teaches. Your ability to chill teaches. Children need to understand how to use these elements as they go out into the world. Confidence teaches. They'll need to communicate confidence as they move about in the world. Bullies seldom attack confidence. A strong, confident mind defeats bullies.

When you're locked in a power trip with your child (or anyone) and you don't know what to do, remember (write this down): It's all about the moment. Ask yourself, "What answer will work right now?" Make the answer as dramatic as you'd like; then apply the feeling of satisfaction you get from having the answer to the situation at hand—this will help you calm down and let it go (in the moment). Revisit the issue when you're more chill. Do you really need to react the way you have been?

Your energy is a precious resource you may take for granted, and it is granted provided you respect the Source. Power trips stem from unbalanced energy trying to force its way in a particular direction. When you balance your energy, miracles follow. Could you use a miracle right now? The energy issue looms every day. Sometimes you feel up to it. Most times, you're just slogging through. Do you know what makes the difference and gives you the energy? Your love for them. Children are living lovelines. Even when your child is a pain in the butt, the love thing keeps you in the game. If you're not in check, if you're off balance, your mojo is off. You've been overwhelmed.

Energy is a boundless resource. Among other things, you're electrical, a fundamental property of matter made up of electrons, protons, and positrons manifesting as attraction, repulsion, hot, and luminous. Combine all that with the spiritual aspect of life and you can see and feel the power surge within. One core understanding is knowing you are this boundless energetic being. Just understanding that preempts a lot of exhaustion. That exhaustion, in turn, becomes a thing of the past and is replaced by a state of tranquility for the hero you are.

Remember this: You are your child's hero. They're looking to you to show them the way to handle things. "Things" include the self, others, circumstances, situations, challenges, bullies, etc. When you consider it, there is no way to handle it all except as the fountain of peace. Otherwise, you lose your mojo and drive yourself to distraction.

How do you recognize and deal with the ever-looming power trip? You can recognize it in the moment by keeping an eye on your feelings. The moment you feel off balance, you know you have something to handle within yourself. It's not coming from outside. Don't listen to your mind playing tricks on you. There is no outside. You produced it all. No one is out there.

"I'm interested in the hows and whys of human communication. Hollywood is 1,000 percent that—almost more than talent. There are agents who only say good things because they know it produces oxytocin."

~ Brian Grazer, American Film Producer

You need to draw on that "endless love tap." You know, like a beer tap? A love tap. Sit quietly and just feel it fill you up; then respond to whatever power trip is in front of you. I suspect you're not doing a lot of that or you wouldn't feel so stressed.

In my mid-fifties, when my son was sixteen, we had power struggles over him helping me around the house. I wanted him to follow some processes and procedures because it was the way I was taught to do whatever it was.

I was dog tired, mentally and physically drained, because business wasn't doing what I needed it to do, and my son wasn't doing what I needed him to do. My lack of power in my business translated into power trips and struggles at home, where I felt I was entitled to the power. But I ended up feeling even more drained and withered.

Process and procedures aside, if there ain't no juice in the line, the lights won't come on. If the results you're looking for need 440 volts and all you can muster is 110 volts, you need some serious rewiring. Rewiring is easy. My favorite means of doing it is meditation. What do you do to give yourself that extra jolt of love's electrical energy?

Being too busy to meditate leads to problems of all kinds. Forgetting to meditate leads to all kinds of problems. Fortunately, I remembered, began to meditate again, and restored harmony to my home.

As you know, different situations call for different levels of engagement. Choosing one's battles becomes important for reserving your energy for 440 volt situations. Don't use 440 in 110 situations. That's inefficient. Efficiency is key for preserving the self, energy, esteem, and nerves.

What if you don't deal with these power trips/power struggles effectively? Well, what do you think will happen? How many out-of-whack parent-child relationships do you suppose are out there? How many have you witnessed? Are you engaged in one right now?

You may be constantly having to deal with individuals who clearly have ego-based power issues. Globally, such people range from terrorists to schoolteachers. Remember this: When we get everyone on the same page, harmony ensues. Working together can't happen without harmony. Nationally and locally, it's the same thing. It's just closer to home. Home is really everywhere. Love is the four-letter word to use most often, and you must mean it, especially in places where there is no space or time. Peace and love go to hell when power struggles are the priority. That's not what you want.

Know when to save your breath. It's not necessary to badger or say the same things over and over again when you have already laid out the whys and wherefores. Silence speaks in more than one way. In fact, when you're silent, communication is happening. The words you spoke before resonate. If you've said them three times or more already, you don't have to say them again. You just need to *be* as you would if you were waiting to see the result of having said them.

Not only do your words resonate in the silence, but the voice of God also echoes in their heads. Your voice, the voice of God, their own egos chiming in—the kid has stuff to work through. Give them some space. Give yourself some space. And remember, power trips make for bruised egos, hatred, and resentment.

The pull cord of negative feedback needs to be cut when talking to your children. Frame your instructions, lessons, and feedback in loving stories and examples from your experience. Are you good at that? If not, get good at it.

EMOTIONAL ABUSE IS DAMAGING AND RAMPANT

Your parenting results are a reflection of who you are. If you received emotional abuse as a child, and you feel anger, anxiety, and/or depression you can't get rid of, you may be experiencing post-traumatic stress disorder (PTSD). Anger, anxiety, and depression are varying degrees of the same thing. I remember trying to talk with someone I thought was my friend about mine, but I could see she was irritated by the conversation and regarded it as an excuse and some form of weakness on my part. (She wasn't a friend after all.)

Sometimes you reach out for help and see or feel the person does not believe you or care. Please do not allow that to stop you from seeking help. I buried my feelings again based on her reaction, and my recovery took that much longer.

Emotional abuse of a child is commonly defined as a pattern of behavior by parents or caregivers that can seriously interfere with a child's cognitive, emotional, psychological, or social development. Some parents may emotionally and psychologically harm their children because of stress, poor parenting skills, social isolation, and lack of available resources or inappropriate expectations of their children. They may emotionally abuse their children because the parents or caregivers were emotionally abused during their own childhood. Straus and Field[3] report that psychological aggression is a pervasive trait of American families: [writing] verbal attacks on children, like physical attacks, are so prevalent as to be just about universal.

A 2008 study by English, et al.[4] found that fathers and mothers were equally likely to be verbally aggressive toward their children.

If you abuse your children when they are young, it increases the likelihood they will grow up to abuse you when you're elderly. Researchers Choi and Mayer performed a study on elder abuse (causing harm or distress to an older person), with results showing that 10.5 percent of the participants were victims of "emotional/psychological abuse," which was most often perpetrated by a son or other relative of the victim.[5] Of 1,288 cases from 2002 to 2004, 1,201 individuals, forty-

---

3 Murray A. Straus & Carolyn J. Field, "Psychological Aggression by American Parents: National Data on Prevalence, Chronicity and Severity." *Journal of Marriage and Family*. 65.4 (2003): 795-808. Jstor.org/stable/3599891

4 English, Diana J. et al. "At-risk and maltreated children exposed to intimate partner aggression/violence: what the conflict looks like and its relationship to child outcomes." *Child Maltreatment* 14.2 (2009): 157–171. doi:10.1177/1077559508326287

5 Choi, N. G. & Mayer, J. "Elder abuse, neglect, and exploitation: Risk factors and prevention strategies." *Journal of Gerontological Social Work*. 33.2 (2000): 5–25. https://psycnet.apa.org/record/2000-05812-001. Accessed December 7, 2023.

two couples, and forty-five groups were found to have been abused. Of these, 70 percent were female. Psychological abuse (59 percent) and material/financial abuse (42 percent) were the most frequently identified types of abuse.[6]

So, you see, what goes around, comes around. I shudder to think what those numbers are today, after the pandemic. In your own best interests, what can you do to halt the physical and emotional abuse of your child(ren)?

To what extent do you understand what you are communicating?

SUMMARY

Your tiredness and its underlying silent killers (anger, fear, anxiety, etc.) may be driving a wedge between you and your family. Look now to see how this may be happening. Covering up alcohol and drug abuse will damage more than just your health. Your example sets your child up for this problem as well. Power trips and emotional abuse stem from not understanding who you really are and what's really going on.

6 https://criminal-justice.iresearchnet.com/types-of-crime/elder-abuse/elder-abuse-by-adult-children/ Accessed December 7, 2023.

EXERCISE

1.) Which demons are you protecting at the expense of your children?

____

____

____

____

2.) What do you do to give yourself that extra jolt of love's electrical energy?

____

____

____

____

3.) Which stories can you draw on from your childhood to share with your offspring?

____

____

____

____

4.) What can you do to halt physical and emotional abuse in your home?

____

____

____

____

Chapter 13

DISCIPLINING AND RESPECTING

"No one would have crossed the ocean if he could have gotten off the ship in the storm."

~ Charles Kettering

Issues with disciplining a child can sometimes make you wish you could just chuck it all and go. Very few of us would be here if parents could get off the parenting ship when things got difficult. Fortunately for us, love causes most of us to stick with it.

In the last chapter, we looked at understanding what you are communicating with your family. In this chapter, we'll examine the discipline and respect needed to achieve your goal of raising healthy, happy, fulfilled individuals.

Get rid of abuse—learn the difference between discipline and abuse.

Abuse is the cruel or violent treatment of a person (or other living thing). Discipline is teaching someone to follow rules or codes of conduct by offering or withholding positive or negative reinforcement to correct unwanted behavior. Disciplining child(ren) is never supposed to be cruel nor violent. Discipline is teaching.

Discipline and respect are two sides of the same coin. To show respect is to admire someone (or something) deeply as a result of their qualities, abilities, or achievements. You and your child are to be respected as human beings, extensions of Source. That's the bottom line. All other abilities or achievements are extra in this regard.

What kind of discipline and respect do you practice in your household?

When Kevin's son was a child, Kevin disciplined him as he'd learned from his mother—yelling and/or corporal punishment. His mother didn't yell much. She believed in hitting first and asking questions later. This model was all he had to go on. This finally ended mid-swing one day as he saw himself doing the very things he hated about his mother's parenting. Is this you?

Another turning point came for Kevin when he felt his son's indifference and coldness toward him. His son was just entering his teens, thirteen or so. Kevin knew the part he had played in creating this coldness, dove into research, and reformed his ways. This interest led him to me.

IS YOUR CHILD DISRESPECTFUL?

Control your child. Some people have issues with my use of the word "control." They prefer "inspire" or "guide" when describing what you do with your children. I agree it can be that simple. However, if I am out at a restaurant or other public place and I encounter parents with screaming, twisting children or kids who are running amuck, "inspire your child" is not the thought that comes to mind. Let's think clearly here. Control is what's needed.

Inspiration is what you do before you get to the restaurant. Control comes into play when inspiration has worn off. Though, I do think they're about the same thing at that point. "Mister, would you please inspire your child to be quiet?" A thorough program of inspiration at home has a lasting effect outside the home, and that guidance feeds the child's decisions for the rest of their life. Your inspiration soaks into them over time. It's too much to expect they won't slip up now and then—and then control is necessary.

A program of inspiration at home includes:

- Teaching your child to meditate. They're still in close contact with Source. May as well help them stay in close contact and get first-hand inspiration. This will also help them become smarter and smarter. You better meditate with them to keep up (wink).
- Catch them doing something right and praise them for it, *often.* Generally shoot for four or five positives for every negative directed

toward them. Our minds tend to remember the negatives. More positives are needed to offset this human flaw.

- Apologize to them when you are wrong. (Keep being wrong to a minimum.)
- Affection and attention are key. Giving a lot of both attention and affection communicates "You're worthy." If they can't get your attention in a positive way, a negative way will do. They flat-out *need your attention.*

BALANCE YOUR PARENTING ACT WITH OBJECTIVITY

Teens are destructive when their pain has been ignored for years. Is your parenting act balanced? A by-product of ignoring negative events in your child's life, especially between one to five, is unsavory behavior in their teens. Einstein said, "We cannot solve our problems with the same thinking we used when we created them." The same is true here. You must rise above the problem to view it properly and then dissolve it. This is done through meditation or other quiet contemplation.

When the washing machine was invented, we stopped washing most of our clothing by hand. When the dishwasher was invented, we stopped washing most of our dishes by hand. When schools cropped up all over the land, we sent our kids to school instead of home-schooling them. Why? Because with all we have to do day to day, it was and still is too much to do *all* that on our own. Same deal with saying the same things

10,000 times or more and nagging. Stop it! Save your breath and shift into the intelligence and wisdom you have accumulated from when you were their age.

If the kids are fighting each other or you, then SLLR (stop, look, listen, relate). Have everyone SLLR and go to their corners for extended periods to first be silent. Then consider how the other feels/felt and what they gain by being (whatever they were being). Help them think through the long-term effects of their actions, not just the heated moment. List the obvious and what they don't see—have them do this on their own as well. Ask, "What thoughts are in your mind?" Instruct them, "If the thoughts feel bad, stop them." Have them start controlling and directing their thoughts in a loving direction. Then have them talk to each other. You and your co-parent do the same with each other. Do only a few rounds of this "talking through" over time on the same subject.

Save your breath. Look fervently for and pay attention to good behavior. Ignore bad behavior (don't even look at them) or use extended isolation (time out) for age-appropriate periods. Do this calmly and with ease.

KNOW WHERE YOUR CHILD IS AT ALL TIMES

Get a picture in your mind of the wonderful person they will become as an adult. You can be inspired daily by that picture. It helps keep you sane, but you must get them to adulthood. You need to know where they are at all times. Teenagers get more freedom, but it can get pretty expensive for you (and them) when there is no check on their freedom. You knowing where they are is their safety net. World dangers are a big, obvious reason for knowing where they are, but a less obvious reason is the parent-child connection itself. There is subtle protection in this connection, a sort of mental and emotional love tether that gives the child a subtle (or not so subtle) feeling of support when they're away from home and an added measure of self-esteem.

Get 'em to adulthood in that vision you have of them. Your vision is of them happy, healthy, and successful. The teenage years help both parent and child to gradually wean themselves of each other, but until then, how do you keep track? Have you instilled enough discipline and wisdom in them so they make correct decisions when you're not around?

"A key distinction when wanting to access knowledge from the superconscious is to use it to help find knowledge that expands upon existing knowledge that can be made sense of to solve current challenges you're facing."

~ Adam Higson

I say own up to this hero position you've gotten yourself into. Break out of "perfection" mode. Claim who you are and make corrections. Connect with the Divine Source to gain the clarity and energy you need to carry out your heroic duties.

ARE YOUR CHILDREN GETTING A RISE OUT OF YOU?

Children get a kick out of getting a rise out of their parents. Why is that? Well, attention, on any level, is what they need. New humans *love* engagement with their parents. If positive attention is not happening, negative attention will do just fine. Child behavior is largely about recognition and getting attention to fill a need they have that they often cannot name. The tricky part is disciplining yourself to give attention in ways that are the most nourishing for your little bio-identical replicas. When you understand the buttons your children are pushing are your buttons and you are responsible for disarming them (the buttons), the whole dynamic in the tone of engagement with your children shifts. Whether you are whispering sweet nothings to them or explaining the laws of the house, you then stand (with new insight) as an adult with mature power who inspires cooperation and respect. (They already love you.)

The button generator is your childhood.

Examine your buttons. I've been taking a good look at myself and my buttons, and I tell ya, I was once a frickin' computer keyboard of buttons, a veritable twenty-story elevator panel of buttons. Just let me be a little too tired to take responsibility for my reactions and my son's ears would singe—for starters. I'm much better these days, thank you, but clearly I used to be overwrought for naught. It always worked out better for me to engage in calm adult maturity. Stretch a disagreement with your child into a shouting match and they'll lose respect for you. Remain calm instead and follow through with the appropriate immediate action: ignore them on the spot. Isolate them on the spot. Ground them on the spot—ice cold, no chaser.

"Comfortable suffocation" is being bombarded by everything that is bad for you. You're wading through all kinds of stuff to find the best for yourself and your family. It's exhausting. Give yourself a break. Meditation helps you to engage as a conscious parent. Conscious parenting reduces stress and promotes good health, happiness, and fulfilled children. Envelop your role as a parent with a strong mind and velvet heart. Do you worry your kids won't like you? Remember, they are not your friends. They're counting on you to get them lovingly, safely, and confidently to adulthood. They'll like you then.

BRAIN TRAINING AND CORPORAL PUNISHMENT

Whooping (whipping, whuppin') was considered strong discipline when I was a child. On occasion, I was invited to go select the tree branch to be used to whip me. It was rather common in the South to offer this (so generous of parents, aunts, uncles, and the like), and if I came back with some little twig, they'd send me back out to get a larger one as often as needed until I got just the right one. I, personally, received only two or so strong whoopings by the time I was nine and decided that was enough. Being on my best behavior from then on was a priority. I wanted no more of that.

I once watched a Dr. Drew show on TV on child behavior problems. It talked about discipline and corporal punishment. 'Twas very interesting because he had quite a wide spectrum of guests on the show, professional and otherwise, who spoke from different perspectives. It was a reset button for me because, at the time, I tended to approve of corporal punishment.

The assertion that stuck with me from the show is when you strike a child, because their brain is still forming, it causes a contraction in the brain that slows brain growth. Not only that but the reptilian fight or fight part of the brain gets bigger and the expansive, inspired, thinking part contracts—the thinking part of the brain shrinks every time the child is spanked! Thus, a pattern of low self-esteem, depression, and underachievement is created. Besides, corporal punishment teaches children violence is the answer. You may cling to the idea that spanking isn't violence, but hitting is violent, so....

The guests indulged in the usual conversation about cultural differences and norms and so forth, but this brain thing hit me between the eyes. If there was ever a reason to tread lightly with corporal punishment, this is certainly number one. Some experts on the show offered their publications as resources for alternatives, such as withdrawing something the child wants, etc. You can find tons of information on disciplining your children differently out there. Different styles of discipline will appeal to different parents...but geesh...their poor little brains...*your* poor little brain....

I know going back a generation or maybe two, most adults were spanked (or whipped) as children. Let's pause for a moment and think about our brains. How much smarter, more relaxed, generally gentle, and happier would we have been had our parents had the means/ temperament for optimal discipline without inflicting pain? Is that even possible? Would America be the superpower it is today? Would we be part of Russia now, or would we have influenced global peace and love? Hmm.... Where do you think the line is between responsible parenting and child abuse? What are your thoughts on this "brain training"?

CHARACTER DEVELOPMENT: TEACHING RESPECT

"What you do speaks so loud I can't hear what you say."

~ Ralph Waldo Emerson

Character (mental and moral qualities distinctive to an individual), education, and development in loving directions are sorely needed today for young and old alike. The young, in particular, suffer from an acute need for self-respect. I add in older adults because they are the parents of these errant personalities who would bully a senior citizen and/or their peers. Is it a lack of self-respect? Remember, we are reflections of each other. There but for the grace of God go I. Remind each generation that they will be seniors or perhaps in need of courtesy someday. Pay in what you want to get out.

The definition of character I'm referring to is: 1) the aggregate of features and traits that form the individual nature of a person, 2) moral quality or integrity, and 3) reputation. It is this aspect of our nature that defines our manners. The degree to which we have high, positive levels of character renders our environment and personal interactions anywhere from hellish to heavenly.

If a child (male or female) is taught to give their seat to an elderly person or pregnant woman in private and public places (lines, buses, trains, etc.), it is unlikely that same child will find it prudent to bully the elderly or others. Good manners and respect are taught by the example of how you behave. Model correct behavior and then teach it. Have the child demonstrate the lesson by taking them out for practice and finding practice opportunities. Once this is done, periodically ask them if they surrendered their seat or turn in line (or what have you) when they come home. Asking serves as a reminder and reinforcement. You can ask, "Were you able to help a senior, pregnant woman, or disabled person today?" "Did you surrender your seat to someone out of respect today?" "Did you hold the door open for someone today?"

"Practice random kindness and senseless acts of beauty."

~ Anne Herbert, Peace Activist

Character development includes showing your children how to "practice random kindness and senseless acts of beauty." Can you name a senseless act of beauty? Examples: giving the shirt off your back or shoes off your feet to someone, feeding a hungry person, paying the toll for the car behind you, etc.

Modeling respect to and for your children builds character. It's a way of kissing yourself. Pass on loving reasons to show respect and the "golden rule-ness" of it all. Ideas and examples of how your and their feelings are affected by being shown respect help to instill this value in your children. Have them practice showing respect to each other as you reinforce the lesson by showing them respect. So much goes into making your world a pleasant place to live. The heart of which is, "Do unto others as you would have them do unto you." You must magnify empathy in your children if you are to save yourself. Do you actively teach your children the golden rule?

TEENAGERS

Poor manners and rudeness are not the only things proper discipline and respect help your child avoid. A *New England Journal of Medicine* study found, "More than 4,300 people aged nineteen and under died from gunshots in 2020, up 29 percent over the year before—and the figure is likely to grow."

Teenage gun deaths, motor vehicle deaths, drugs, and disease all vie for first place. When it comes to driver distraction, cell phones play a significant role. Distracted drivers are the leading cause of car accidents.

Adult drivers (yes, that includes parents) and teens have equally bad driving habits. Where else would the kids get it? Here is yet another place where we go on automatic. We place our precious meat suits inside metal and fiberglass missiles. All or many of us, together, at one time, move the missiles onto the road at varying speeds and then decide it is okay to take our eyes off the road and surrounding vehicles—to use the phone. We use the phone, comb our hair, eat, drink, all manner of madness. Do you do this?

This has to stop. I'm driving out there. Think of *my* safety! You might hit me. For everything you hold dear, this has to stop. The number of teenage deaths alone from distracted driving rivals that of total deaths from gun violence. Snap to. Being and remaining fully conscious and alert without distraction while driving needs to be the example you set for your children and the center of learning to drive. It's not just good etiquette. Distracted driving is not cute. When you do it, it just shows how unconscious you are. New humans, also known as teens, have a lot of "I am free" and too little "This could kill me." Your kids are chips off the ol' block. They're doing a replay of that ol' song of defiance you used to play for your parents.

As for gun violence, I don't know where to begin. I'm already over my word limit for this book. Let me just say, a gun is the sort of dangerous tool that attracts its purpose to it. Mental illness and emotional stress are rampant in this country. In the face of this fact, the prevalence of guns in our society is the same as saying our/your life/your children's lives don't matter. Inaction, as a people, is condoning disaster. You are far less likely to attract gun accidents and death to yourself and your family if your focus is loving and life affirming. When guns are not part of your household, your life, you are actively engaged in attracting the opposite of what guns serve.

What do you think of your disciplinary measures and respect for your child(ren) after reading this chapter?

SUMMARY

Discipline and respect are two sides of the same coin: the adherence to discipline and respect of the child to you, and your loving application of discipline and respect of the child. It's important to engage in teaching and showing the harvest a good attitude provides. Pause in the morning, look in the mirror, and give yourself praise for the great job you're doing as a parent. Do you do this? What do you say? Do it every day.

EXERCISE

1.) How do you point out the harvest a good attitude provides to your offspring?

____

____

____

____

2.) How do you stop yourself when one of your negative triggers is activated?

____

____

____

____

3.) How do you maintain your alpha-ness without bullying?

____

____

____

____

4.) List three ways you handle a difficult child without stressing yourself or them.

____

____

____

____

5.) List the ways your offspring get a rise out of you.

____

____

____

____

____

6.) What is the latest lesson in respect you modeled?

____

____

____

____

____

7.) How do you feel about corporal punishment and brain training? Did this chapter change your attitude?

____

____

____

____

____

8.) Name a few senseless acts of beauty you can practice with your kids and have them practice.

____

____

____

____

____

Chapter 14

GETTING ON THE SAME PAGE AS YOUR CO-PARENT

"Fortunately, perfection is not a requirement for creating great relationships."

~ Dr. John Gray

Great relationships can be had with ex-lovers, ex-spouses, and co-parents. To a large extent, media and society has programmed the hate relationship with exs. It is not necessary to have it, and it doesn't serve your health nor the health of your child(ren).

The last chapter was about discipline and respect. In this chapter, I encourage you to be on the same page as your co-parent as you apply discipline and respect.

If you have a co-parent, what do you suppose is important about their existence in your family?

CO-PARENTING WITH THE EX CAN BE A PAIN

Your child comes home from their weekend with your ex and reports that someone there, an adult, hit them. You don't know the person. Your ex does.

I'm reminded of a time when I was in a fever to confront a woman who hit my son while he was visiting his father.

I went to her job the next day and waited for her to get back from break or lunch or wherever she was, but she never showed. My ex assured me he had handled her and the situation, but still, I was uneasy with my son visiting him from then on. I had other reasons for this uneasiness, but I won't put the man's business out here right now.

At the time, I was dealing with the personal devastation of separation, pending divorce, and having lost everything. It was a little difficult for me to separate reason from rage most of the time. Know what I mean? What reaction and actions are appropriate in infuriating situations and which are not? It was all a blur to me. In general, my co-parenting experience was pretty mellow except for the part where he paid no child support. My mother had my brother's father thrown in jail for this offense. I was too frazzled to go that far.

What issues are you dealing with when it comes to your co-parenting situation? Is it smooth running? Do you get along well? If you are not together, are you on the same page with your ex-partner when it comes to parenting your child(ren) regarding discipline and respect? If you have a good system going in this regard, count yourself blessed.

"Men and women are so different that we'd be better off if we actually spoke different languages, because then we wouldn't think we were communicating."

~ Kimi Avary Fallon

So many struggle with co-parenting. Some let flat-out hatred of the ex get in the way, hold a tug of war over the kids' affections, and/or don't comply with custody agreements. The kids cleverly play mom and dad against each other. These are just a few of the problems with all their variations and flavors. No one wins in these scenarios. Remember: The child(ren) in the middle of this have unresolved feelings. No one can win until they can resolve their feelings, and that may take years.

Let's just say the sooner the parents get their act together, the faster happiness happens for all involved. I'm reminded of a couple of dear friends who got divorced after about seven years of marriage. This was before I started my parent coaching practice. From what I understand, the husband got the seven-year-itch and had a couple of affairs, and the wife couldn't put up with it. Their kids were seven and three at the time. Cute as buttons. With all the ensuing yelling, screaming, and fighting, I saw the kids change before my very eyes. At the beginning of the separation and divorce, the cuties became depressed. This can be expected because the mom was depressed and they lived with her, plus they had their own unresolved feelings to contend with.

Once the divorce was final and the parents could see what they were doing to the children a little more clearly, their love for the children won out and they came together in co-parenting. I'm not saying I saved them a lot of unnecessary heartache, but things changed when I pointed out to them separately their attitudes were toxic to themselves and their children. As soon as they changed, the children thrived.

So, why talk about this? I want you to recognize who you are in this scenario. When you stop in the moment and remember your humanity and the humanity of your ex and your children, you can release significant pressure from your heart. You can begin to heal yourself and everyone involved.

"Men have trouble knowing what women need, because women have a hard time expressing what they need in a way that men can hear."

~ Kimi Avary Fallon, Conscious Couples Network

Hurt feelings, anger, or hatred must be allowed to flower, wither, and die. Often, the feelings won't be denied, but they can be recognized for the destructive entities they are and truncated. Your health and happiness depend on doing so. Tools to help eliminate the co-parenting with the ex problem include meditation, yoga, remembering your humanity, recognizing there is no fault in either of you (this may take some doing), regulating and extricating negative emotions, and maintaining a clear channel to your Divinity.

If you feel disconnected from The Divine within, all sorts of problems ensue. Co-parenting difficulties will just be one of them.

What if you decide to continue with the status quo (if it is a bad one)? If it's your comfort zone and that's where you're comfortable, your desire is to be respected as a matter of your humanity. Just remember that the toll your decision to stay in a bad state takes on your health and the happiness of your offspring will be felt by the rest of us because we are all connected. Surely you don't want the responsibility of all that, do you? Haha; I'm casting a wide net here, but it is true. Just as a loving stone cast in the waters ripples out into ever more loving waves, so does the sick, negative, and hateful.

STRESS IS KILLING YOU

"A typical stress reaction, which most of us experience countless times each day, begins with an avalanche of endless biochemical reactions in your body."

~ Dr. Jon Kabat-Zinn, founder of the Stress Reduction Clinic at MIT

Stress is deadly and preventable. In America, every second, 3.5 people die because of stress. Single people and non-parents are stressed too. As an emotional being, your health is tied to your emotions, your child's emotions, and the family's emotional energy. You must keep your emotions healthy. Healthy emotions yield a healthy mind and body. You have a right to long-term health and happiness. Your happiness and joy level feeds your well-being and your whole family, emotionally, mentally, and physically. You are here to show your baby humans the ropes, so to speak. First, you've got to learn them yourself. Then show them, the babies, how to maneuver successfully in this world we have all created.

Slogging through the day-to-day painful and stressful issues in parenting and our society is not fun. You're here to have fun. Having to say the same things over and over again, having anxiety over being the authority figure instead of your child's friend, paying the bills, and being disrespected while you're trying to be respectful are intense stress factors. I learned having even the mildest anxiety and fear simmering beneath the surface day in and day out is the same as walking around with a thirty-pound weight in each hand all day, day in and day out. Can you see how hard that is on the body? Is it any wonder people age prematurely? Can you see how you can practically predict when age-related illnesses will strike?

I was a stressed-out, miserable mess of a parent for a very long time. It was only through the active pursuit (and finally capture) of solutions to my life issues that I freed myself from the worry and stress that plagued me. Conflicts with separation, divorce, self-esteem, and overwhelming money issues all colored how I parented and moved around in the world. The truth is, you don't need to see where these problems come from. You need to nip them in the bud. It's not necessary to recount the nitty gritty origin of every nitty gritty thing. It's necessary to turn your attention to the inside, to the Ultimate Source, and melt some stuff off. Thirty years ago, I perceived being a parent as a bad practical joke being played on us unsuspecting, single, free, and childless women. Men can often abandon their unborn offspring or fly the family coop whenever they want. Women, not so much.... The main thing is to understand no matter how it looks, your co-parent is possibly experiencing killer stress as well.

ALIGNMENT TOOL: CHILDREN

I have observed and heard parents complain that they and their spouse are not on the same page when it comes to discipline. Often, one or the other is the disciplinarian, and that person is more structured and consistent in what they say to the children and what they have them do. That's wonderful until the other parent comes in and tells the child, "You don't have to do that," or "It's okay to do/have/etc. that," undoing the disciplinarian's instructions. This is confusing for the child and disrespectful of the co-parent. The child is not getting what they need (to learn a lesson). They need structure and predictable consequences for their behavior, good and bad. Disrespecting the co-parent stains the parents' relationship. The disrespected one harbors resentment, expressed or not, that festers and grows emotional pus.

For the love of your spouse and the strength of your children, cut that crap out. Parental discipline is not the place to play some sort of twisted good cop, bad cop game with your child. It is not the time to try being your child's friend. Suck it up and be a strong *adult* role model for your family.

Do you play good cop, bad cop with your kids? Parents, get together without the child and work out your home curriculum. Children are a major alignment tool for couples. Determine which methods of discipline you will use and in which circumstances and, by all means, do not contradict each other in front of the children. This is one of the times where you are one. United. Don't argue in front of the child about disciplinary tactics. It frightens them. They feel responsible for the fight—which promotes guilt or some sort of sick power-playing from the child both parents can do without.

Contradicting a disciplinary measure set for your child by the other parent does not help. Both parents need to be on the same page. Power and love are joined in mom and dad. Be as one when disciplining your children. Work with the other parent to come up with acceptable and effective disciplinary measures you can agree on.

Can you see and feel now why it's important to be on the same page as your co-parent?

SUMMARY

When co-parenting with your ex, keep a picture of the ideal positive relationship with them in your mind. Connect to the good feeling this picture provides. Maintain this feeling when you interact with them and in how you talk about them with/around your child(ren).

EXERCISE

1.) What kind of relationship do you have with your co-parent?

____

____

____

____

____

2.) What do you do to maintain balance in the relationship between your ex and offspring?

____

____

____

____

____

3.) What can you do to rid yourself of negative feelings (which are stressful) about your ex?

____

____

____

____

____

4.) How are you playing good cop, bad cop with your kids?

____

____

____

____

____

Chapter 15

FINANCING YOUR FAMILY (RAISE THE CHILD AND THE DOUGH)

"A bank is a place that will lend you money if you can prove that you don't need it."

~ Bob Hope

Let's look at money. What are you doing to finance this eighteen-year parenting project? If your kids are adults, where did this love excursion leave you financially?

In the last chapter, we talked about getting on the same page as your coparent. In this chapter, we look at raising the child and the dough.

I was a walking mess of denial after separating from my son's father.

Social worker: "I see here you have $2,630 in savings."

Me: "Yes."

Social worker: "You must spend all of that before we can give you food stamps and assistance."

Me: "But that would leave me with nothing."

Her: "That must be done before I can help you."

Me: "You mean to tell me I must be penniless before I can get help?"

Her: "Come back when you've spent it all."

If you can see and feel the weight of the financial stress you're enduring, know that I understand and have been there. You're strong enough to carry it, but at what cost to your health and well-being? Are you a walking mess of denial?

NEWS OF TODAY: YOU'RE OUT ON RECESS

Recess doesn't just happen at school. Many parents are out on recess—refusing to come in from the unconscious state fear and stress has put them in. Look at today's economic environment and headaches? What about the stress of all that on your back? Unfortunately, this particular problem is not new. It's age old and persistent. Get over it already.

How do we get over this problem? If we step back and observe, we see that in spite of this problem, we are still here and have persisted through many years. Some of us settle into a "what's the use" attitude and remain in the financial class of our parents or lower, and some, against all odds, rise above the family legacy.

How that is done is not technically a secret anymore. If you dig for the answer, as I did, it can be found. I have an interest in people accessing these answers. Recess is over. Some of us just didn't hear the bell. It's time to recreate yourself as a financially responsible parent. There is a line in consciousness one crosses that allows not only an easier time raising children, but helps enhance all aspects of life, even making money. It's a spiritual yeast that expands you in all directions. Thrilling events result when you tap into this part of yourself in earnest. Are you ready to come back from recess?

> *"Whether the successes you want to achieve are personal or professional...physical or financial...whether you want to change the world or simply be happier (which, I believe, changes the world)...the person who can do it is already inside of you."*
>
> ~ Brad Yates, Emotional Freedom Technique (EFT) Expert

RAISE THE KID AND THE DOUGH

Children are known to be one of life's most expensive experiences. From birth to age eighteen, we're talking approximately $300,000, and that's without private school and college. It will probably be twice that by the time your kids have their own child. Thank goodness we don't have to cough it all up at once.

Let me help you with this particular problem. All money issues are rooted in the same dirt. Let's scoop 'em out and burn them: You need to surrender to the aspect of yourself that is the hero, the Divine.

Raising children does not require too much money. Too much money is waiting for you to be clear and claim it. That is the real problem. You have access to "All Abundance." We all have equal access. Oprah Winfrey doesn't have more access than you. Bill Gates doesn't have more access than you. Nor does Warren Buffett. It's a matter of allowing yourself to thrive. Tension perpetuates lack.

Parents tend to water-down their dreams as time goes along. What dreams have you watered down? Raise the child and the dough. Simply saying the task costs too much will make it so. Cut it out. Your thoughts, feelings, and words have power. Children arrive on the planet powered up. They are an evolving seed containing the power of its own expression (as you are ever evolving). You are to guide and protect them in a moment-to-moment way without creating the drama of future doomsday scenarios that involve, "OMG, I don't have enough money." They are "blessing reinforcements" and inspire you to be your highest self. They require you to give them—as much you as you can—the loving you, the patience you, the wise you, the you who has time for them. You are the gold, the diamonds, the real treasure in their lives. (Kiss your right bicep.)

When you find the sweet spot in your mind and consciousness, you gain access to all abundance, Source. The question becomes: What kind of abundance do you bring forth? Abundant money is extremely helpful and available, but if it happens that only Abundant Love is available to be tapped, know that no finer gift from you can be given, no finer usher into adulthood can be made.

HOW MONEY WORKS

Have you ever wondered about how money works? First understand "the setup." The top one tenth of one percent have wealth set up, from this country's founders to Davos (the town in Switzerland where the World Economic Forum decides every year how much more of the pie they'll keep). The other 99.9 percent of us get to play by the rules those at the top set, and all we can do is make the best of how money works. Now that you understand the setup and know what you're working with, what can you do inside it?

My interest in parents understanding how money works stems from a natural curiosity in childhood about why some people appear to have way too much while others have way too little. I went about learning as much as I could about this phenomenon.

My interest especially grew over the last twenty years or so, with me eventually getting four securities licenses and a life insurance license, and it culminated in realizing different people care about understanding how money works at different levels. Ascending these levels is based in a few simple concepts that, had we been taught them in school, would put us on target for a comfortable retirement today (if we're not already). The following are the basic rules of how money works.

First, when is retirement age? Retirement age is any age you are when you have the money to retire. It could be eighteen. How long do you plan to live? The longer you live, the more it will cost on an exponentially expanding expense scale due to inflation. Answer this: How much will you need to be comfortable in old age, come what may? Do you know what that number is?

You need to know four basic things about how money works. They are:

1.) The Rule of 72
2.) The Tax-Advantaged Growth of Money
3.) Tactical Offense and Defense of Your Money
4.) Debt (the Rule of 72 used against you) is a central cause of stress and (preventable) chronic disease

Let's look at each one briefly.

The Rule of 72: This rule is about how money doubles, and it goes like this: Take the number seventy-two and divide it by your rate of return. (The annual rate of return is the percentage change in the value of an investment. The interest rate is the cost of debt for the borrower and the rate of return for the lender or investor.) The number you get is the number of years it will take for your money to double once at that rate of return.

For example, if you're getting a 4 percent rate of return, divide seventy-two by four and you get eighteen. A 4 percent average rate of return will double your money once in eighteen years. If you're twenty-nine and have $10,000 (the principal investment) you've just put in a conservative stock portfolio gaining an average 4 percent per year and you don't touch it, eighteen years later, you'll be forty-seven and have about $20,000. In eighteen more years, it will double again, so at sixty-five, you'll have $40,000. How do you feel about that?

Now imagine you are getting an average rate of return of 12 percent over time in an aggressive stock portfolio: seventy-two divided by twelve equals six. Now your money is doubling every six years or so. At forty-seven, you have about $80,000, and at sixty-five you have $640,000. The difference between 4 percent and 12 percent is the amount of risk you are willing to take.

The Tax-Advantaged Growth of Money: What is this? I don't mean tax-deferred like IRAs and 401ks where you eventually pay taxes on the money and potential gains. I mean tax-advantaged funds through the use of Roth IRAs and/or certain life insurance policies. You pay tax on the initial money deposited and then can access your growing cash without paying taxes (within certain guidelines).

Tactical Offense and Defense: If you understand sports, you understand what offense and defense mean. If you work with some proven tactical money managers who practice active money management, you can realize higher rates of return on money. Tactical managers watch money moment to moment and attempt to move it out of harm's way when the markets start to go down and move the money back into the market when the markets start to go up.

What happens when something you value goes on sale? Let's say your favorite sweater from Nordstrom costs $400 and goes on sale for $50. What do you do? That's right. You buy more in every color.

When money goes on sale (the market goes down), though, what do most people do? They do the opposite. You should be buying when money products are "on sale" so when they go up again you win. Both strategies (tactical and passive) have benefits and risks.

Why does all this matter? The idea is to accumulate enough money before retirement (or whenever) and after the kids have flown the coop to live on the annual interest of the accumulated principal of your investments and not have to touch the principal investment asset (best-case scenario). You then move the principal into passive management, "buy and hold" conservative accounts, where the money stays invested in the market through the ups and downs. Once you retire, it's good to have the money you've accumulated placed in conservative accounts. Then they don't gain or lose more than 3 or 4 percent per year, something bearable.

Debt: Debt uses the Rule of 72 against you, compounding interest in favor of the banks, credit companies, or whomever is charging you interest. If the creditor is charging you 28 percent, they are doubling their money on you every two-and-a-half years, meaning you'll owe them more than twice what you originally borrowed, depending on what you've paid on the bill without adding more to it. When you add in their service charges, annual fees, and monthly finance charges, your real interest rate could be 35 percent or more. It is best, of course, to pay off debt completely every month. And remember, good credit scores reduce the interest you're required to pay.

FLOWING MONEY

Oxen work, humans create. Humans create "in flow." Would you like to flow money faster than you need it? Get in sync with that idea.

As a child, I was constantly told no when I asked for something because we had no money. Always no. I remember thinking, *Can't do nuh'thin'!*

When Christmas rolled around, my brother, who was four years younger than me, would receive a gift or two, but nothing for me. My mother would tell my stepfather as a compliment to me, "She's old enough to understand we have no money. She's a big girl."

This poor finances scenario was drummed into me. One day when I was in my early twenties, I went to a training session put on by a couple of guys—I wish I could remember their names. They introduced me to maintaining a silent mind rather than constantly worrying about money. In short order, financial abundance ensued. They offered to continue working with me. I declined, saying, "I think I've got it." I thought, *Why continue to pay them when I have it already?*

Well, the answer was that the force of habit and distractions will take you out and land you where you were before. Having consistent support and/or coaching is helpful for eliminating that slip and fall.

What do you suppose happened? Not long afterward, sometime around 1982, I got in a financial jam, again. A strange sort of amnesia had set in. Crushing debt was weighing heavily on me again. I hadn't had a real estate deal in months. I said, "Okay. This it. I'm sick of this recurring problem." I turned off the TV, radio, music, all outside entertainment, and applied meditation and the silent mind (again). About a month later, I created financial miracle after miracle until I was so powerful I scared myself. I would say, "I want two deals this week," and two deals would happen. I was giddy with joy and said, "I want three deals this week," and three would happen.

Then one day, I got out of bed and couldn't feel my feet. I walked to the bathroom, looking down at them. They were there, but I couldn't feel them. I got dressed, went to work—I was "floating." Then I got scared and it all stopped. I felt the lightness draining from my body. I understand now that the depth of my conscious connection to Source was very clear and made me very light, which is why I couldn't feel my feet.

Shortly after allowing this fear to set in, I married badly, gave birth, and separated. I was devastated and lost everything. The turning point for me was, as I neared homelessness, friends took me in for a few months. I reactivated my spiritual practice and dug myself out of yet another financial hole. My friends gave me three months to get up and out. I met that.

"Within all of us is a divine capacity to manifest and attract all that we need and desire."

~ Wayne Dyer, American Writer

My question here is: Do you constantly forget who you are and thereby cause a constant slip and fall cycle, or have you not fully realized who you are? Please wake up to who you are and get off of the hamster wheel of suffering. I know it's not easy, but it can be. As I write this, I remember how money flows when I remain in my right mind, the silent, powerful one. I urge you to remain there as well...and teach your children to do the same.

"Be thankful for what you have; you'll end up having more. If you concentrate on what you don't have, you will never, ever have enough."

~ Oprah Winfrey, American Entrepreneur

The above quote is true because as an "Extension of Source," your power is operating all the time and expressing itself through your feelings; therefore, when you feel anything, you get more of what you're feeling, good or bad. If you feel love and prosperity always, you get love and prosperity. If you feel hate, jealousy, or lack mostly, you get hate, jealousy, and/or lack. What do you feel most of the time?

LET GO AND RECEIVE

A Meditation quickie:

> Are you feeling crazy? Full of dismay? Despair? Stretched too thin?
>
> Please know that buried in your walls of flesh is a glowing light of power and peace waiting for you to tap into it.
>
> Sit now. Close your eyes. Breathe.... Breathe.... Breathe.
>
> Know Source is there radiating peace, prosperity, and unimaginable power. Relax into it.
>
> You are naturally powerful. Release fear. It only attracts more fear.
>
> Grace is your natural state. Return to it now. Regain efficient functioning.
>
> Visualize and then create the world you want for yourself and your family. Recognize your co-parent, brothers, sisters, and children as your co-creators. Release the idea of better than.
>
> Release competition. It's a manmade construct.
>
> Breathe.... Receive abundant wealth, abundant health, abundant joy.

How do you feel about your ability to finance your family's life now?

SUMMARY

Raise the kid and the dough. You're gonna need the dough. Make a point of understanding how money works—it's empowering. Understanding your role in letting money in (or not) is also empowering. It's about how you feel about it.

EXERCISE

1.) How honest are you with yourself about how you handle money?

____

____

____

____

____

2.) Why do you suppose you don't have enough money?

____

____

____

____

____

3.) What are you doing to work the rules of how money works?

4.) What do you feel most of the time about money?

Chapter 16

CREATING YOUR CUSTOM FAMILY SYSTEM

"Life brings us all big and small storms that can keep us from experiencing total joy. We can be a bit more like the eye of the hurricane, unaffected by the chaos around us."

~ Shelly Lefkoe

In the last chapter, we talked about money. This chapter is about creating a family system that, as in Shelly Lefkoe's quote above, helps you be a bit more like the eye of the storm, keeping your sanity in this lifelong journey and these chaotic family times. With a family system in place that gives you and your family more consistent peace, you may not be totally unaffected by the chaos around you, but you can get pretty close to being unaffected.

As a parent, I flayed about from one survival scenario to the next, never fully appreciating nor understanding how precious the first eighteen years are. I had no example or sense of this as a child. Having a meaningful system of self- and family-care in place would have tremendously improved all outcomes for myself and my son.

All the previous chapters built the foundation for creating your custom family system. The family system you create sets your family's priorities. A family system is a set of principles or procedures working together to produce an organized and peaceful home. Creating your custom family system entails using the elements we've discussed—peace, your core values, integrity, discipline, and respect along with your unique family processes and traditions. The following six sections are observations about variables that influence your family system. Then we'll dive into building your system.

MAKE NEW FRIENDS

When it comes to being a parent, you must remember you are the parent. You are not their friend. You are the chancellor and dean of Home University. You set and pay for the curriculum, play activities, and devotionals. Understand and appreciate that what the child learns at home is what sustains them (or not) at the core of their being for the rest of their lives! Sounds serious, doesn't it? It is. It's serious, and it's also extremely beautiful. Love makes provisions for everything you need. You help your child(ren) cultivate their loving nature to help advance the human race. It's a God thing.

You need friends because they, like your children, reflect how you're doing. Most importantly, they are sounding boards when you try out ideas. They support you emotionally when you go through rough patches. Friends revel in your successes and bring you chicken soup when you're sick. Your child(ren) is/are to be spared this responsibility. They're not qualified to be your friends. It handicaps them if you place them in the role of friend. If you are so insecure as an adult that you feel you need your child as a friend, you need to stop that nonsense immediately and get professional help. If your discipline of your child is weak, inconsistent, or non-existent because you don't want them to get mad at you now or when they become adults, get professional help immediately to free yourself of these faulty feelings. Do not weigh children down with the weight of your adult insecurity. Find adult friends to talk to.

You are not your child's friend. If you find your child talking to you disrespectfully, as if you are their friend or on their level, you have only yourself to blame. It is an early indicator that you have been lax in your role as dean, chancellor, fearless leader, and protector of all things beautiful and sacred in Home University.

SETTING FAMILY PRIORITIES

During family meals around the table, you gather and distribute love to each other—even if there is discord, Love is there, gathered around the table...looking at itself.

The world has always been full of distractions. Children have always been drawn to the new thing, whether it be a type of music, television, video games, wars, sex—okay some of these are just new to them. One of the best ways to keep up on what's new and ensure these things are filtered through your values is the family meal.

Make it a priority to have as many family meals at the table as possible each week with everyone present. During this time, share information and have conversations. Get a feel for what they're feeling and what you're feeling about what they're feeling. It's a point of connection, one I regret not fully capitalizing on.

OBSERVE WHAT THEY REPEAT

An addict is one who abandons themselves to something compulsively or obsessively. Are you addicted to your cell phone or other tech appliances? Would you rather look at a screen than your little human? What's a great alternative activity to teach your offspring instead of staring at their phone?

Your children's needs include protection from the influence of violence. Is your little one propped up next to someone playing violent video games? Are they watching *John Wick*? Does their football coach push them to crush their opponents? Do they find you watching a twenty-four-hour news network that relies on dispensing hate and calling for violence against anyone who disagrees with them? Teaching and learning require repetition. What negatives are your child(ren) being exposed to repeatedly? It stands to reason that repetition teaches both positive and negative behaviors.

HOME IS WHERE THE HEARTACHE IS

"When the student is ready, the teacher will appear. When the student is really ready, the teacher will disappear."

~ Lao Tzu

Home is where the heartache is. When your child leaves home, heartache moves in. How will you know what your heart needs? You will feel it. Who is the student? Is it the child, or is it you? There are no accidents, none. That's right. That's what I said. None. Your children show up on time and in time with the lessons you are to learn. So, get down to the business of learning. Lesson 1: Be in the moment. Lesson 2: Be patient. Lesson 3: Be attentive.... Be.

Man! I wish I had mastered this information before my son was born. I actually thought I was supposed to wing it. I had the forethought to think if I waited until I was older and more mature, I would have all the wisdom and knowledge I needed to raise a child—and so I waited. I waited, not knowing the roots of the heartache and insecurity from my childhood had not been removed. I reached a magical age preordained by hormones that said, "It's time," and I went forth and multiplied.

My friends, again I remind you parenthood is a serious eighteen-plus-year project. You have to pick up the mantle and engage as a life coach. You train your children for greatness as you're being trained in grace. After eighteen years, you're still a parent, and if you've done your job, you'll have sufficient time to rest and enjoy a month-long vacation—and an additional eighteen years of enriched wisdom and exquisite relaxation stemming from their unleashed freedom as adults. (Hahaha, just kidding.)

Heartache, in its many forms, is something to strike against before it can show up or, at the very least, get a hold of your feelings. When you prepare yourself and your children for life's challenges, happiness, and joy, you're fully loving moment-to-moment with them, even when they misbehave.

MULTITASKING

Multitasking is harmful to your health and brain. Do you multitask? Do you train your kids to multitask?

Training kids to multitask has been proven to be not only inefficient but also detrimental to your and their health. In the past, and for many even today, multitasking has been regarded as the thing to do. It *seems* to make sense that if you can do one thing in a certain time, then doing two or three things in that same period is even better. I specifically remember one (or more) bosses I've had over time saying employees who can multitask are the most desirable. I could literally feel myself and the other employees in the room "gear ourselves up" to impress the boss. This kind of thing was and probably still is a deciding factor when it's time to lay off people—who multitasks the best, who is willing to do more than one job, who handles the stress of all that the best?

Well, I can tell ya the science is in and it's clear—we can only do one thing at a time. The only time multitasking works and is not stress-inducing is when a machine does the second and third tasks. A human's conscious attention is singular and pointed. We attempt to multitask because our mind is inherently inclined to stress us out. But the brain can only do one thing at a time well.

When we are teaching our kids, we often tell them to focus on one task at a time to do each well. Why do we have them do that? We do it because we know it's the best way for them to excel in whatever it is they are trying to do. That goes for us as well. Just because we are grown up does not mean we can handle multiple tasks (distractions) and do any one of them 100 percent. Our strength in adulthood is focus, which is the laser sharpness with which we can focus on any task or challenge. That is the muscle we want to develop in our kids. From there, the Theory of Relativity was born, Olympic medals are won, and beautiful books of poetry are written....

So, if you're pressing your kid to multitask, cut it out! You're setting them up for unnecessary stress over tasks they would otherwise enjoy.

What's your take on this aspect of training kids?

YOU TOLERATE TOO MUCH

Do you tolerate just way too much? Let's say you're catering to ungrateful family members—your significant other, kids, parent(s), siblings—and about to scream. Save it. It's really not about what they are doing or not doing. The pandemic and its aftermath aren't making life any easier, and it wasn't easy before the pandemic. You may feel stress and despair mainly because you tolerate way too much. You're tolerating it within. Once you sort it out from within, everything starts to change for the better.

Do you think you must remain buried in endless confusion, burdened by your accumulated responsibilities, and that life is just what it is? That's just not so. If you just use the power within to your advantage more, you will free yourself from tons of stress and disappointment. For example, I encountered a lot of back-talk from my son when he was a teenager, backstabbing from my coworkers and the people on my business team, and overwhelming worry about a significant pile of debt. Since I had neglected my meditation and visualization practice because I was "too busy," it was equivalent to taking my eye off the ball in a game. When you do that, sometimes you get hit in the head.

"Half an hour meditation each day is essential except for when you're busy. Then a full hour is needed."

~ Anonymous

I restarted my meditation, visualization, and prayer practice. My feelings were soothed. At some point, I noticed my son and I were getting along, my debt started to melt, and fun returned. Forgetting or neglecting your centering practices of meditation, prayer, and visualizing what you really want, gets you in trouble with your happiness bubble.

YOUR FAMILY SYSTEM

You jump up out of bed, frantic because you're late for work. The kids are up, have made a mess of the kitchen, and are running and screaming all over the house as you try to corral them and get them to dress for school. The dog's barking, your spouse has left for work, and your client is calling to find out where you are. It's chaos.

In parenting, we need a family system to squelch the chaos, restore order, and enhance integrity.

Are you in denial? Are you parenting by default?

You may feel at peace with your parenting, but do you understand what you've made peace with and how it affects the ultimate outcome, the adult your child grows into? If you have a family system that renders the best outcome, you have a healthy relationship with the strong, happy, independent adult you hope to raise.

When my son was a child, my skills as a parent were poor. They were half bad to start with and suffered from divorce and the loss of my business. Many factors during his childhood devastated me to the point where I knew if I did not get myself together, I would leave a legacy of depression and pain to my son. Have you been through that level of degradation?

The main reason for creating and maintaining a family system is to keep your sanity as you grow your child into a strong, happy, independent adult. Chaos rules when you're unfocused, compromising your integrity, and have weak or nonexistent family systems. Stress then begins to eat away at your mental and physical health. Remember: According to the Centers for Disease Control, seven people die from stress every two seconds!

Here's an example of a parent who was "stress walking." I volunteered at my son's middle school. When you get to hang out regularly at your child's school, you get to know who the trouble-making kids are. One child was known to be very disruptive. One day, I was in the office when his mother arrived. She banged her fist on the counter. "Where's the principal, you m*****r f*****rs!" she demanded. The principal came out and ushered her into his office. Everyone in the office could hear her yelling. Then she left saying, "I don't have time; you figure it out." The principal said something I couldn't quite hear. The parent responded, "My son did no such thing!" I thought, *That child is exactly like his mother*. Talk about mirrors and reflections! Geesh.

A system helps in integrating the core values you want your family to adopt. Do you like the idea of having done a good to excellent job of raising your child(ren) or, if your child is an adult, of healing parenting wounds you may have inflicted on your adult offspring? Having a family system in place allows an all-encompassing and comprehensive means of family administration that overlaps with preventing or addressing pain in adulthood. It's a reference point for your offspring when they become adults and parents themselves.

As you know, people tend to parent as they were parented or, in some cases, they make a point of making significant alterations to their parents' parenting styles. Do you value and appreciate what you've already done as a parent? Do you feel your offspring does?

How are your adult offspring treating you? They can't help but love you. Do they like you? If they're adults, do they come around? Call you? Do they share funny stories of how your influence manifests in their world?

Gerald (a newly minted adult) told me a funny story (well, funny to him anyway) of how he was driving a car full of his buddies to Las Vegas when a couple of them got into a beef. I can't remember what he said it was about, but he said he heard himself sounding exactly like his dad, Ron, saying, "If you guys don't stop all of that fussing and arguing, I'm going to turn this sucker around and head back home. I mean it!" Then he pulled the car off the highway and had them all get out. He told the two arguing gents, "Come to some agreement and apologize to each other. I'm not making this long-assed trip in a car to Las Vegas to get there and be miserable." They put their disagreement aside, apologized, and a good time was had by all. Gerald said he was amazed at himself and how he felt like the only adult in the car. (They were in their twenties.) He told Ron, "Dad, I could hear your voice in my head as I was giving them the ultimatum! Thank you for that."

Even when you are working on a specific issue, other parenting woes clear up when you have a system. Your problems don't happen in a vacuum. In fact, when you operate in a true vacuum, Source rushes in to fill it with something you want.

START WITH THREE STEPS

"Try as we might, we cannot force our children to reach their full potential. Theirs is the life that they alone must live. The role of the parent is to prepare the most fertile soil and appropriately water the seedling so it can most fully blossom."

~ Gabriel Cousens, MD

The Family System has three core steps and some steps within the steps. For our purposes, I'll do the summary. You can add or subtract as you see fit. At the head of the system is (are) the parent(s). The parent(s) set the family priorities, determine the core values, and are responsible for mapping out and communicating the family system to the child(ren).

Make a point of:

1.) Being peaceful as a parent. Relax into a parent mindset. Build ease and relaxation into your experience as the parent so your role as hero can be executed with fun and finesse. Don't look back on the days when you were single as somehow better. This is a new day. Embrace the noise and chaos when and if it comes as part of the fun. Are you okay with adding more fun and ease to your parenting? If so, relax; most things are not that serious. Understand being a parent is a calling. Eliminate the fear and anxiety so it is easier to integrate your parent mindset.

2.) Teaching self-control, efficiency, and orderly conduct, also known as discipline, is a high priority, as is respect, both child to the parent and parent to the child. To feel honored and esteemed is a deep and extremely important need in humans. It goes both ways. Do you agree? Understanding and appreciating this core need is expressly taught in the home. Bring it to the fore in your family system. (I distinctly remember noticing I was more courteous to people outside my home than to family. Family is closer and speaks to what's really going on with you.) The result will be more peace because your family gets recognition, yourself included. More joy will be present. You intuitively understand why this is so.

3.) Raising the kid and the dough. If money and supporting the family is challenging, get to the root of this problem within yourself. You establish the foundation for family prosperity. Would a legacy of your offspring "knowing how to fish" be all right? Do you know what I mean by that? It's the old feed versus teach trope where teaching leads to a lifetime of eating instead of just one day. Teach your kids how money works as they grow.

What if you don't use a family system to help in parenting? Then you're attracting more than usual random chaos. In some households, chaos reigns. If it's a problem in your home, you are stuck nagging and begging, saying the same things over and over and over again. You get to keep the anxiety of being the authority figure. The ever-looming money issues continue to haunt your very existence and the mounting stress of all this prematurely ages you, makes you sick, and then sends you to an early grave.

Is your family like a boat without a rudder, roaming aimlessly on the sea of life's circumstance? Do you want to risk your offspring being rendered groundless, without a firm foundation to secure them in the storms of life? When would *now* be a good time to bring your best to the fore? Hoist anchor and row in.

So, how do we quell the chaos in our parenting brought on by parenting by default and filling in the blanks by guessing? The Master Parent System is a good start.

THE MASTER PARENT SYSTEM

"General Systems Theory, a related modern concept [to holism], says that each variable in any system interacts with the other variables so thoroughly that cause and effect cannot

be separated. A simple variable can be both cause and effect. Reality will not be still.... Relationship is everything."

~ Marilyn Ferguson

The purpose of a Master Parent System is to help organize the activities of home life, enjoy parenting more, and bring more peace to all involved—which wards off premature aging, chronic disease, and family chaos, thereby transforming parental stress into peace.

The quote above by Marilyn Ferguson (author, editor, and public speaker known for *The Aquarian Conspiracy*) speaks to the strength of each family member's connection to every other family member. It's an electric connection. You can't see the energy, but you can feel the power throughout the family.

I like to think of this system as being diamond shaped. Families are the crown jewels of society, so I feel diamonds represent this well. You are being forged into diamonds by grace through the use of heat, pressure, and the weight of time: the heat of the day-to-day dealing with children, the pressure you face in supporting the family, and the unrelenting march of time that makes you feel you're not doing enough fast enough.

Having a family system helps you build expertise and integrity as a parent as you go along. You gain greater insight into what causes issues. Overall, you gain confidence, expand your parenting skills, and learn to make parenting easier on yourself and your offspring, thereby preventing stress and passing along stress to your child(ren). Create action plans that reinforce your family system.

Master Parent System: (*Please refer to the implementation details in the respective chapters.*)

I.) Peace in being a parent (it's a calling).
  a.) Relax into a parenting mindset.
  b.) Acknowledge and eliminate your fears and anxieties.
  c.) Integrate your parent mindset.
  d.) Practice silencing your mind, meditation, and visualization.

II.) Discipline and respect—two sides of the same coin. Stop saying the same things over and again. Begin to look for and pay attention to loving behavior only.
  a.) List and systematically instill your family's core values and priorities.
  b.) Communicate these values and priorities to the family with integrity via example.
  c.) Talk in a way your child will listen.
  d.) Get on the same page as your co-parent.

III.) Financing your family life. (Tension perpetuates lack.)
  a.) Raise the kid and the dough.
  b.) Learn and teach how money works.
  c.) Flow money—connect with the energy of money.
  d.) Let go and receive.

Optionally, create a custom family system and map. (Which items in the above lists do family members do for themselves, each other, and the household? Draw it out (and then do it in map form with the kids.)

a. What do members do for themselves and when (at what age)?
b. What do they do for each other? Address respect for feelings also.
c. What do they do for the household and when (at what age)?
d. Recognize your tribe. Build in rites of passage and when they will occur. What do you do to celebrate each?

CREATING YOUR CUSTOM FAMILY SYSTEM MAP (with your child(ren) if they still reside with you)

"When you organize your life, you change your life."

~ Heather Sontag, Serene Space Organizing

For fun, gather the kids and create a piece of art illustrating your family system to put on a wall for everyone to use as a guide, reminder, and reference. This step can also help to save your breath. You can have the family refer to the map or collage on the wall when they need a reminder. You can use it to reinforce duties/chores and schedule rites of passage celebrations.

Generally recognized rites of passage are graduations from one level of school to the next, *bat mitzvahs*, etc. Some schools even celebrate graduating from kindergarten (so cute). Build on these and have your own in-home celebrations to help drive home the idea that they have accomplished something, adding to their self-esteem. Character development is part of rites of passage from one stage of development in childhood to the next, right on into adulthood. Once children hit certain marks, highlight their new responsibility for themselves and to the household with a ceremony or celebration.

For example, at age four or so, they can start straightening their room and cleaning up after themselves. When they are preteens (ages ten to twelve), give them lessons in doing their laundry, then have them do it. And as teens (ages thirteen to seventeen), they can do laundry for the whole family. Perhaps they can learn to cook simple meals for themselves as a preteen and progress to participating in cooking whole meals on the weekends, something you can do together. Teaching children can be fun, and it's easier when you share some of your best stories from your childhood and make a big deal of rites of passage. They learn how to care for themselves (and others), they gather self-esteem, and as time passes, it gives you a break from having to do... *everything*.

Celebrations can be your usual party in addition to being creative with special outings and ceremonies that speak to what makes *them* special. Get the siblings involved in delivering praise to the sibling being honored using their own words. Being a good parent is to be commended and celebrated as well. How do you honor and recognize yourself for being a good parent as their growth stages and rites of passage are marked off? (Parents can do this privately with/for each other.) Build some fun into this. Treasured memories are the sweetener in your tea, the cream in your coffee, and the soft whispers of love in the wind in your old age. Treasured memories also feed the family's self-esteem.

Have you established a system your family can run on?

SUMMARY

Having a family system in place helps you be a bit more like the eye of the hurricane, unaffected by the chaos around you (if there is any). As the chancellor of Home University, you establish the curriculum and guide the implementation, directing what is learned in your home. The Master Parent System is a mode of building in relaxation and ease into the curriculum as the center of operations in the individual and the family as a whole.

EXERCISE

1.) What priorities will you set for the smooth running of your home?

____

____

____

____

2.) What are you tolerating way too much of?

____

____

____

____

____

3.) Write down one or more childhood experiences or rites of passage to share with your child later.

____

____

____

____

____

4.) Which rites of passage are celebrated in your home and how?

____

____

____

____

____

Chapter 17

BEING PARENTS OF ADULTS

"Parents are the centre of a person's solar system, even as an adult."

~ Justin Trudeau

Trudeau's quote above acknowledges something often overlooked. Let's talk about the unsung parents—parents of adults. If you are the parent of an adult (or many adults), you may be experiencing any number of emotions related to the stage you are in, from empty nest syndrome to being the grandparent of adults, and how good a job you feel you did in raising them.

In the previous chapter, we looked at creating your family system. In this chapter, we focus on the experience of being a parent to adults.

DO YOU GIVE THANKS FOR YOUR DIFFICULT CHILDREN?

Do you give thanks for your trials and tribulations? Parent pain doesn't stop (for many) just because your child becomes an adult.

For instance, let's look at the emotional challenges Niki had even though her son, David, is an adult. Once David moved out on his own, she invited him to dinners for holidays or just to see him. In the beginning, he would stand her up, or when he did show, grudgingly, he'd make a point of arguing and recounting how she had failed him. The evenings always ended with her in tears and crying herself to sleep. He always pointed out some blaring imperfection in discipline or some other error of hers he would grab onto mid-visit; then he would twist it until her night was ruined and she felt miserable. Niki knew this was the fruit of having left his father and taken him with her when he was six, along with poor communication skills and corporal discipline. He couldn't forgive her for that. After a few years of these types of visits, she'd had enough. She'd done the best she could with what she had at the time. It was time to forgive herself and his unforgiveness. It was time to let go. She no longer invited him to dinner. Who needed the grief? She was much happier. As time passed, his attitude shifted (because hers had). He "grew up" a little. They enjoy meals together now, mostly (though she's not always sure of how he is feeling afterward).

Holidays are particularly potent for the awakening from hibernation or incubation of the seeds that expand your greatness. Your challenges and difficulties often heighten this time of year because the people you love gather energetically and physically around you (if you're lucky) and activate those seeds. As they germinate, you can choose to recognize the challenge or difficulty and transcend your usual pain. *Learning to transcend is the gift of difficulty.* Otherwise, your growth is stunted. Face the fear that you may lose your child forever if you let them go. Fear keeps you trapped in unhappy circumstances and endless quarrels. You're worth more than that. No one, not even your offspring, is worth that trouble. Like the old railroad safety crossing: stop, look, and listen to what's really going on. Then find solace and solutions in meditation, divine radiation, and visualization.

Here is a process I recommend to remedy this problem in the moment when bad feelings come up:

1.) Stop the moment you feel the first twinge of discomfort. Breathe. (That's right. You need to start paying closer attention to yourself... and your breath. You spend way too much time externally, reacting to the external.)

2.) Relax in the moment. Detach and de-escalate as you breathe. Observe what's happening in your body as you breathe.

3.) Assess your most appropriate reaction from this calmer state.

Later, when the triggering moment has passed, take time for quiet reflection and investigate what's going on with *you.* Pinpoint the thing and begin to extricate it through meditation, ho'oponopono, or whatever your method for clearing and cleansing your emotions. My big guilt trip was, "I am a flawed mother, so I deserve this abuse." I am so glad I sought and found solutions to that feeling through meditation, etc.

If you're the parent of an adult, the chaos may simply be the noise occupying your mind, the residual effects of what you perceive as your parenting mistakes and/or your desire to have a friendship with your offspring who don't want the same. Let go.

STRESSED? HIT A WALL?

"The time to relax is when you don't have time for it."

~ Sydney J. Harris

Have you stopped long enough to reflect? Have you ever hit a wall in your activities, in your harried parenting and work-life schedules? It's more than okay to hit the pause button and come back when you're refreshed.

The last nine months of 2017 dictated that I reflect. It was precipitated by a friend saying (when I told them my grand plans to schedule multiple group meetings over the summer), "People aren't around during the summer." The moment I heard that, I was deflated. I was exhausted from having put on an online video summit and doing most of the work myself. I hit a wall. I noticed some time later, though, the freeways and grocery store lines didn't support the statement. My reaction was really all about what was going on with me at the time—too much work, overscheduling, and late nights.

That statement gave me tacit permission to not be around. I took the time to look at my business' activity over the preceding ten years and evaluate what really mattered in a prolonged, focused way. When was the last time you did this? I had worked myself into a grease spot that was slowly evaporating. Know what I mean? I gained many extra pounds working until the wee hours of the morning, rarely stopping to exercise.

During this period of reflection, I employed quite a lot of meditation. I gazed into the different aspects of my life—parenting folded into view, and I was able to see my son (now a grown man) couldn't possibly understand me. Yes, I expected him to. But I had a significant head start in years on him. I needed to stop my unreasonable expectations of his thought processes. The parent perspective always needs to consider and be mindful of the offspring perspective.

Do you need to stop expecting your offspring to fully understand where you're coming from? We all have a certain amount of nearsightedness when it comes to our parents and trying (or not) to understand their perspectives, my son to me, me to my mother, your offspring to you, and so on.

I saw that I needed to reclaim my sovereignty (such as it was). Many parents of adults need to reclaim their sovereignty, their supreme power over themselves. Step back and remember your most powerful and free self before parenthood. Have you done this? Who were you? Were you someone you liked? What would it take to get back there again? Engage meditation or whatever your instrument of introspection is and remember this person. Reach back and bring that most-free you forward into now.

Embrace that you. Take many moments to cherish and appreciate that you. Re-embody that you as you heap on your current wisdom. Leave out the controlling, clingy, and guilt-ridden parent you. Now. Don't you feel better? I'm constantly refreshing and reevaluating what's happening in my life. Are you? What would it take to stop long enough to give yourself and your family the treasure of the relief you gain from introspection and meditation? It could be a dinner conversation or a few.

When you've engaged your mind this way, peaceful solutions begin to occur to you. Some solutions simply happen without you having to do anything. Isn't that a much better quality of life?

"A 1 percent annual reduction in the level of four health risks—weight, blood pressure, glucose, and cholesterol—has been shown to save $83 to $103 annually in medical costs per person."

~ Centers for Disease Control, 2016, (for employers)

How are you doing with stress? Have you stopped long enough to reflect on possible natural solutions to your issues? Do you feel you can't afford to do that?

"Sleeping less than four hours a night, according to the research, was the equivalent of aging your brain almost nine years."

~ Western University Brain & Mind Institute

Can you afford not to engage solutions? Your mind tells you reasons like "money and time are tight." The truth is that money and time are constructs we've all bought into and need to put on hold when they begin to intrude on our and our family's health and happiness. How do you put the constructs of time and money on hold? The best things in life are free. When you meditate (which is free), you enter the timeless realm where everything is possible. When everything is possible, money becomes possible.

"...80 percent of premature heart disease and strokes are preventable."

~ The Centers for Disease Control, 2016

Eighty percent! To put time and money before your health and happiness is the same as putting the cart before the horse, the tail wagging the dog, running before you can walk—you fall on your face, hit a wall, and become stressed, sick, and unhappy. When one is sick, they are often unhappy. If you are unhappy, sickness is forming or already happening.

Myriad issues are involved in being a parent (even of adults) that have a kaleidoscope of solutions. At the heart of all these issues and solutions is the ever-abiding presence of peace. Peace is central. It's a by-product of meditation. Peace garners patience, no matter what the parenting/personal challenge is. Your offspring are here to help you master patience in a deep and abiding way. This continues when they are adults. They may not be there physically, but you are.

Fear is the underpinning of impatience. It stands to reason that eliminating fear opens different views into the kaleidoscope of solutions—many solutions offer relief even if you're not a weary, stressed parent. For instance, my subtle fear was that my son didn't like me. When it became obvious that he didn't, I was deeply hurt. After all I had done for him (most of which he couldn't possibly know), how could he not like me? The parent's perspective must always consider and be mindful of the offspring's perspective. When you disagree or find yourself in an argument with them (or anyone), put yourself in their shoes. It can be a stretch sometimes, but if you see the event as happening to you, it can temper your response in a way that leads to desired outcomes.

Here's a fun exercise: Put yourself in the shoes of everyone you encounter today (or whenever you're out). The split second in which you do that will immediately put you in a state of peace because at that level of awareness, you are engaging in empathy. The first thing you'll understand is you cannot know what the person has gone through that day or any day. Next, all you need to do is offer understanding in your mind. They don't need to know you're doing it. If you have a kind word, share it. Then notice how you feel.

In meditation and reflection, I realized my subconscious fear was that I'd lose my son forever. Guess what? That was a fear I had to let go. Losing him forever is a very real possibility in this physical realm. It's life. It rendered me clingy, and you know what happens when someone is clingy. It brings about the very thing you fear. So, if it's to be, why help it materialize? Why eat your health with this fear? You have to hit the reset button and refresh.

Another example—you, as the parent of adults, have guilt over the way you treated your offspring when they were children. It's the same guilt as mine. So, what do you do about it now? Here's a solution: Enter that place (in meditation) where there is no time, money is not needed, and all things are possible. Wash yourself in the quiet of this place. Let your possible happen.

Are you trying to ignore the wall you've hit, you know, continuing to slog through without stopping and reflecting? Are you using pills, alcohol, drugs, or neglect of yourself to get temporary relief and saving real solutions for when you get time? Please stop. Source deeply loves you and wants the best for you. What is the best for you? Use the meditations suggested in this book and deposit your question in Quiet Mind. Meditation is the single most powerful thing you can do for yourself and your family.

HEART PROBLEMS—CONTEMPT FOR PARENTS

Do you suffer from parenting guilt because your offspring turned out to be "a bad guy," in prison, or some such situation? Do you have contempt for *your* parents? Heart problems often start once the kids are grown. I've taken a bit of time out to assess my objectives, and I've come away with a startling conclusion. I feel like a fraud. I have to say it. My so-called advice and wisdom on child discipline comes with more than a little regret. My own son alternately seeks my advice and counsel or holds me in contempt. I've had to take the time to sort out why this is. Here it is:

For those of you who have minors still, just know that when they grow up, they become who *they* are. It will be tempting to blame yourself for their and your own perceived shortcomings. Banish the thought!

American psychology researcher Judith Rich Harris says, "genes and outside-the-home environment have a greater influence than parents on children's personality development."

Think of your influence and the environment you provide as a parent as being up to about 70-80 percent. It's an intuitive thing I have that informs that opinion and most of this book; it's not science, as far as I have been able to find, yet! The remaining internal kernel of 20-30 percent is what a parent has no influence on. You can only hope the 70-80 percent of your good influence holds sway. For all the molding and building you do as a parent, the fact remains that you are merely the usher, the conduit of the future as your parents were for you. Love your humanity, your parenting, warts and all.

Why do you let your offspring's negative stuff run you? These phantom fingers of pain and guilt are nothing more than the mind noise you allow to sap your energy. There are so many other, better things to do with your time and energy: there's money to be made, homeless families to help find food and shelter, animal rescue operations with which to volunteer, campaigns to save the planet, trees to plant, and local church drives of various sorts to support. The list is nearly endless! The key word here is "allowing." Don't allow it to sap *your* energy. Remember: You are the boss of you!

I know, I know. You like wallowing in that "love" thang, but once your offspring are adults, you need to take your "separation exercises" seriously. You need to inject Joy into your activities by remembering what you loved to do before you had a child or what you've always dreamed of doing but never had the time to do. Make the time for it now! Heaven forbid you have boomerang offspring (adult offspring living with you) or are suffering from empty nest syndrome (you're grieving your adult offspring having left home)! Hopefully, you're not having to deal with a lot of lip and attitude. That would definitely be adding insult to injury, so to speak.

Can you get any comfort or insight from your experience at that age with *your* parents? It sometimes helps to pull that memory up and be as honest as you can about what was happening then. Are there any solutions you can glean from that memory? It can be quite amusing to remember your attitudes from back then. It can be even more insightful to remember your parents' attitudes! What did they do right that you can use? Do you want to use it? What did they do wrong?

All in all, I say you need to guard your health through it all. The premature aging thing is getting a bit ridiculous. Let's halt that ugly soldier in its path. There are way too many of us stressed and wearing stress on our faces and bodies! The good thing is, if you can see it, you can make haste to do something about it. The bad thing is many of us think that look is normal. It ain't. Do as Elsa in *Frozen* says, "Let it goooo." Peace of mind is an option and a choice. Choose it. It may seem glib in the face of what you're going through, but I assure you, it can be done. Learn how to let it roll off of you like rain on a duck's back. If it's more like a storm than just rain, please do go within. Come within, out of the storm. You are not alone. You are placed here on earth to have fun. Somewhere through the generations, that purpose got lost or completely forgotten! Bring that *back* to the front of your mind. Dance with that idea. Revisit your twenties if you think that will help. Your heart is yours. You must protect it! Let's forgo heartache and heart problems.

JOB WELL DONE

Your grown child recounts how you "didn't let them get away with it" and how that made them stronger. You may have found that just because your child is now an adult, it does not mean all stresses and "being a parent" issues subside or fall away, never to appear again. On the contrary, the stresses are still there and even more vexing because the child is now an adult and no longer has to listen to you! Isn't that a rather revolting development? I like the idea of being revered as a parent. How about you? Do you like the accolades that come with a job well done? Do you value being appreciated—not as the pillar of all wisdom—but appreciated? You are not satisfied with just settling…for the stress, anxiety, and illness, are you?

So much of our lives have been wrapped up in raising our children that, for many of us, it's hard to detach. You may be suffering from PTSD (Post-Traumatic Stress Disorder). A great many parents are suffering from PTSD and don't even know it, or they have lingering Post-Partum Depression Stress! Why was I walking along the streets picking up cigarette butts…to smoke? What brought this mother to that level of degradation? Devastation from divorce, parental pressure, and the loss of everything! *Being a parent* is one of the unrecognized onsets of PTSD. Many of us are walking around in a stress fog, wondering what happened. We're experiencing the effects of it, and it's killing us!

Four categories of PTSD exist according to the National Center for PTSD, but the one I see most in parents is: Feeling keyed up (also called hyperarousal). You may be jittery, or always alert and on the lookout for danger. You might suddenly become angry or irritable. For example, you may have a hard time sleeping, you may have trouble concentrating, you may be startled by loud noises or surprise, or you might want to have your back to a wall in a restaurant or waiting room. There are the above and random pieces from other categories like nightmares, flashbacks, and triggers. You may stay very busy to avoid seeking help because it keeps you from having to think or talk about the event (being a parent). You may not have positive or loving feelings toward other people and may stay away from relationships. You may forget about parts of traumatic events or be unable to talk about them. Do you see yourself in any of this?

These stresses wear you down and make you more susceptible to chronic diseases and Alzheimer's. *All of this is based in fear!* What would it look and feel like to relieve yourself of these anxieties and stresses? What are those areas where you say, "If only I could get rid of…(fill in the blank)," or "I wish I could be more confident in…(fill in the blank)," or "I wish I could be better at…(fill in the blank)"? It's not too late to save yourself. After all, you can possibly have grandchildren; you want to be around to see and love them!

Part of being the parent of an adult is being able to detach, assess situations, and view them objectively, offering advice and solutions only when asked and being too busy with your own life to meddle in theirs! Do you have those parts down?

If you are a parent of an adult and you are emotionally clingy, have trouble detaching your feelings from your adult offspring's "business," and think your illnesses are just what happens as you age, it's really deeper than that. If you would just realize that unhealthy emotional clinging to your offspring and the continuing stress from the past is killing you, then you would give yourself the help you so desperately need!

Typical issues parents of adults face are:

- Coping with offspring who are distant or don't speak to them
- Empty nest syndrome
- Offspring who are rude to them
- Anxiety over how they treated their offspring as they raised them and the endless stream of negative self-talk about that
- Wanting to have way more input into their offspring's life than the offspring wants.

Here are the problems with trying to address the above:

- Have you ever noticed how you can see the problems with other parents and their kids, but you can't see your own? You may have blind spots.
- Your growing health problems continue to get bigger.
- Prolonged and continued estrangement from your offspring when there may have been opportunities for reunion or reconciliation.

What are the beliefs that are critical for repairing your anxious heart and undoing your PTSD?

- Know you can gain the proper perspective.
- Actively engage in activities that ward off Alzheimer's disease:
    - One of the great discoveries in warding off Alzheimer's is

frequent ballroom dancing. It's the only physical activity to offer protection against dementia at a rate of 76 percent! It offers the greatest risk reduction of any activity studied, cognitive or physical.

- Doing crossword puzzles at least four days a week reduces the risk 47 percent.
- Reading offers a 35 percent reduced risk of dementia. Bicycling and swimming – 0 percent, playing golf – 0 percent." ~ TAP, The Alzheimer's Project.

- Engage lovingly in your self-care: nutrition, exercise (such as ballroom dancing, yoga, etc.)
- Know you can reactivate a certain aliveness that you've long forgotten.
- Have an awareness of the overlapping and separate destiny your child has as a human.
- Know how to initiate the relaxation response. (Meditation anyone?)
- Know how to create powerful visualizations.
- Know how to turn negative thinking into productive thinking.

Oh! Let's not forget that the adult offspring of divorcing and divorced parents have issues also, albeit on a different level, but no less jarring! The personal grief that consumes some adult children is not to be taken lightly, not to mention their needing to provide possible financial, emotional, and physical support of one or the other parent or both! Is this you, caught in a stress sandwich with your offspring and your parent(s) as the bread? Let go and let God, regardless of what's happening because it is all summoned by *you*. This, too, can be made easier.

WHEN DOES IT STOP? ALL THIS SHIT TO DO.

You've got to go to work in addition to caregiving for yourself, your grandchildren, and possibly your adult offspring, your significant other, and maybe aging parents. You have to cook and do household chores. You feel life is a drain, and you feel hopeless with all that's going on: aging, menopause, office politics, disrespectful family members, unfulfilled dreams, flooding, fires, etc. The Evanescence of Life (the impermanence, the evaporation, the possible expiration at any moment) begs the question, "What is it all for?" I felt those very things starting in my mid-fifties. Since I wasn't ready to check out, I chose *moment-to-moment exhilaration* as my goal. Exhilaration for even having moments and exhilarating moments began to pile up, to accumulate to the point that I realized feeling good and happy is all that matters.

You give yourself all of that, and when the end comes, you're ready, like when you've said all the loving things you could and should have to a dying loved one, and now you *and* they are at peace. When does it stop…all this shit to do…? It stops when you stop it, when you stop seeing your life as a chore and start celebrating every moment you get to do…anything. The *way* you're receiving it (and I admit you're receiving a lot) has *everything* to do with how and what you feel. How and what you feel dictates your stress levels and attracts more of what you're feeling into your life.

Even with meditation, it's reasonable to expect that most of the actual "chores" won't fade away immediately. The key is: *What feeling* are you coming out of meditation with, and to what degree are you maintaining your meditation "high" throughout the day? Can we agree that if you *feel truly wonderful* as you go about doing this litany of responsibilities, it doesn't matter what they are?

By my mid-fifties, I had my fair share of work trying to launch a business, household cleaning, cooking, being mom to an adult, "mean girl" coworkers, and financial and personal responsibilities. I was too buried in things to do to have it even occur to me that they could end. What got me through was meditation and visualization. Since then, most of those things have melted away, and the melt continues. What ultimately matters is I felt good when I would go with the flow in those pressured times. When I stopped focusing on "all those things to do," the problems disappeared one by one. I urge you to deepen your spiritual practice. Stress is not natural. You're more than that.

FREE YOUR MIND AND YOUR ASS WILL FOLLOW

I was bippin' along, minding my own business, when out of the blue, BAM! I married, gave birth, and divorced all within four years! My mind imploded. I felt destroyed.

It was 1987. My life went to hell in a handbasket very quickly once I left my husband. I was too depressed to work, though I didn't understand that at the time. I thought if I kept plugging through, I could go on as usual. Business wasn't happening. It never occurred to me I was depressed. Within four months I lost my bank account. Six months later, the lights went out.

The rock band Funkadelic has a song titled "Free Your Mind and Your Ass Will Follow." Like the song describes, I was in a fog because I couldn't hear myself. I didn't know what to do, or how to do it. With the end of my marriage, I knew firsthand there were no guarantees in relationships.

There was so much noise, confusion, and embarrassment in my head that I could not hear me. Have you ever been there? As they say, "A mind is a terrible thing to waste." This wastefulness has to stop. Are you listening to yourself? I'm not talking about the loud, suffocating noise your mind makes all the time. I'm talking about that "still quiet" voice underneath the noise. Are you listening to that, to "you"? Can you hear it?

Through meditation, "still quiet" gets louder and drowns out the "noise" until you eventually hang out in "still quiet" most of the time. Meanwhile…

- Gain more appreciation for the *relief* that curiosity and presence bring to unpleasant situations that arise in being a parent and in other parts of your life.

- Be more curious, quietly. Appreciate curiosity. It's a function of the mind that promotes your happiness and well-being.
- Write this down: *Presence is a function of my Divinity.* Presence is the thing your mind translates with from the ether, The Greater Mind. Presence is channeled to your mind via your brain. Your brain is a giant receiver. You don't want to waste that. Trust me. Your mind, your brain is more precious than gold, diamonds, platinum, and a host of many other things you give attention to and value!

How are you feeling now about your difficulties having adult children?

SUMMARY

If you're the parent(s) of an adult and you are stressed and have hit a wall, don't allow contempt from your offspring to compound your pain. Acknowledge yourself for a job well done (you got them to adulthood). Free your mind of the noise of yesterday and make room for and relish your capacity for life today.

EXERCISE

1.) How is your relationship with your adult offspring?

2.) Do you feel your offspring hold you in contempt? How?

3.) Where are you in your spiritual practice?

____

____

____

____

____

4.) What do you hear from that still small voice within?

____

____

____

____

____

Chapter 18

KNOWING WHO YOU ARE

"Silence is the language of God. All else is poor translation."

~ Rumi

Maybe you know all these things; maybe you don't. The truth is you are all these things, and you are none of these things. You are *the great mystery* to yourself.

In *A Course in Miracles*, published by the Foundation for Inner Peace, our instruction is "Make no decisions by yourself." This means we're to make our decisions with Source rather than with just the loud noisemaker in our head.

Such decision-making really requires full conscious attention to what your mind is doing every moment because the mind is in constant decision-making mode. Therefore, the exercise, the practice, is to keep it quiet, and it will then be in sync with the Mind of Source at all times. At that point, you are dwelling in the Light of Source. As you dwell in the Light, you start to take on a glow, which is your divinity shining through. You are God. Your godself at this point is heavily influencing and producing miracles! This explains why so many depictions of our Divinity as individuals are of glowing and/or shooting light out of ourselves on a cellular level.

When you realize/know you are in this deep connection with Source, being in joy and being exhilarated are automatic. Therefore, you must remember this connection in each moment so you remain in/radiate joy, where the avalanche of life's abundance pours in to fill you. Yes, the energy is very high.

Enlightenment begins when you start going to silence in communion with Source and consistently make it a deliberate action. You then move on to easily selecting silence and maintaining it, understanding the silence itself is the conversation with Source. All else becomes automatic and easy, period.

You've been looking to connect with the True Source of your power. Choose to make that connection now. You were born into greatness and don't even know it. It's time to end the cycle of pain. End the feelings of depression, rage, anger, and despair. It all ends with you.

"Everything you seek and everything you experience—everything—is inside you. If you want to change anything, you do it inside, not outside. The whole idea is total responsibility. There's no one to blame. It's all you."

~ Dr. Joe Vitale, Author and Spiritual Teacher

This is the context of this book and your existence. You are God. Your child is God. Your parents are God. Their parents are God. *All people are God.*

"Be still and know I am God."

~ Psalm 46:10

The above psalm is a call for you to go within, be still, and know the paradox, "I am God," you are God. Respect yourself and your child as God and, of course, the paradox; know God is God, Source. God's power has no limit—it is greater than ours and all others' power.

Connect to, plug into, your Divine Core. From there, what you need in all forms is fed. From there energy, money, relationships, and health are enhanced beyond measure. What would you do to leverage the Power of the Universe?

How do you ease your pressure? I asked repeatedly over the years what it felt like to "know I am God." I got my answer. I finally understand the concept that "it's all as easy as picking up a pencil." It is the feeling of ownership of creation like that of the God from which you sprang.

Maintain your godhead: Relax in each moment. Tune into all your senses—sight, sound, smell, skin (touch), taste—physical, mental, and spiritual receiving. Surrender to it.

Rest...
Enter peace.
Loosen your joints, muscles, and nerves.
Allow Source to induce...
Xquisite Silence, quiet mind.

When stressed, savor something with each of your senses in that moment (or a moment soon after). Love. Appreciate the ability to savor. Give thanks that you are God. Relax deeper in that knowledge. Repeat.

Perceive your godhead directly with your senses and allow your offspring their God-given right of perceiving theirs. They come here with information. Respect that.

"Fear knocked at the door.
Faith answered.
There was no one there."

~ Old English Proverb

Dwell in the State of God. Surrender to your power.

YOU ARE AN ADULT CHILD

You are an adult infant, a baby in the eyes of Source. You are the Offspring of Source, and when you consider the vastness and depth of that Intelligence, it's humbling and somewhat comforting to know you are capable of the same extreme compassion for your misbehaving offspring as you receive from On High. You just need to chill out. From God's perspective, your children are your siblings. We are all children of God.

SUMMARY

When you practice knowing you are God, all else becomes easier because you are in constant conscious contact with Source, aka God. Choose to maintain this connection. You'll be glad you did.

EXERCISE

1. What does it mean to you to know you are a child/offspring of God?

____

____

____

____

2. How does knowing you have a direct connection to Source change how you parent?

____

____

____

____

____

____

3. Now that you've read this book and done the exercises, how much of a chore is it now to relax?

____

____

____

____

____

____

A Final Note

ANSWERING THE CALL TO PEACE

Your children are not your children.
They are sons and daughters of Life's longing for itself.
They come through you but not from you.
And though they are with you yet they belong not to you.

~ Kahlil Gibran

What are you going to do now? You have read and finished my book. What will you do differently? What actions will you take? What results for your family and yourself do you desire going forward? How are you creating change?

This is a "call to arms," the loving arms of peace and, if so desired, prosperity. It's not enough to have read this book. You must put your energy and attention into truly knowing and practicing what you've read on ever-deepening levels.

I challenge you to answer the call to peace and joy personally, because it affects your family experience. You can read all the parenting and spiritual books in the world, but if you don't apply what you learn to what you need and want, very little to nothing changes. Start now to unearth your true will.

On the six lines below, list six actions you will commit to taking within the next ninety days as a result of reading this book.

1. ______________________________

2. ______________________________

3. ______________________________

4. ______________________________

5. ______________________________

6. ______________________________

In this book, you learned how to have peace as a parent and a person. You learned how to shed/eliminate the fears blocking your joy and peace. You learned how to get what you want and parent at the same time, solve the issue of your child not listening, get a handle on discipline, and teach your child respect. You learned how to put a system in place to avoid a lot of chaos, and as you go through time, running the household will get easier. Oh! And finances—you learned how to raise the dough. You learned how to make your life easier in general. If you apply what you learned, you will truly transform your pain into peace and find being a parent so much easier.

Now that you have read my book, I encourage you to contact me to tell me what you liked about it and what you disliked so I can improve it for the next printing. More importantly, tell me about you, your challenges, and your obstacles and adversities so I can help you. In fact, I am offering you a complimentary, no obligation, thirty-minute consultation via phone, Zoom, or in person (if geography allows) to see how I can assist you.

My email address is Rowena@RowenaStarling.com and my phone is (510) 779-2486, so please email or call me with your name and your time zone so we can schedule your complimentary consultation.

I wish you good luck. I wish you love and prosperity. I wish you all the happiness and joy in the world.

Your friend…

ABOUT THE AUTHOR

Rowena Starling is the CEO and founder of Save Your Breath, LLC, The Rowena D. Starling Foundation, a mother, author, professional keynote public speaker, coach, and philanthropist.

She is an emotional resolution specialist, has two bachelor degrees from the University of California, Berkeley, is a retired investment advisor representative, and has fifty years of extensive training and experience in meditation and what it takes to be happy. She is instrumental in helping mothers eliminate fears and in healing family relationships.

She went from the devastation of divorce, losing everything, and near homelessness to raising a son who loves her, launching a business, appearing on *The Today Show*, *The O'Reilly Factor*, and other national and local TV programs, plus international radio and in newsprint. She now helps women, and especially mothers in their mid-fifties, eliminate stress and aggravation by teaching them to transcend their fears and recover their power.

Rowena's mission is to help mothers and women enjoy their lives more, have more fun, and ward off premature aging, preventable chronic disease, and the chaos brought on by the inherent stresses and aggravation served up to us by society and motherhood. Eliminating fears starts the process.

Always busy, Rowena's current projects include developing The Rowena D. Starling Foundation, serving mothers through liaison with social services, and serving households through liaison with school districts.

Rowena currently lives in Berkeley, California. In her spare time, she enjoys movies, painting/artwork, and long reflective walks.

ABOUT "BE DIVINE NOW" COACHING

If you want to transform your pain to peace or you just want your life to be easier in general, allow Rowena Starling to help you. Your life is the most precious thing you have, whether you have kids or not. When you work with Rowena, you will help yourself boost your energy and connection to Source and attract more of what you really want in your life.

Feeling fear, stress, and being overwhelmed isn't necessary to get the things you want. Let Rowena guide you through the processes necessary to free you. This is done through one-on-one and group coaching calls, unlimited email and text access, and an easy-to-follow transformation roadmap.

Rowena will simplify the process for you, save you time and money, and serve as your coach. For more information, visit one of her websites listed below and/or text your name, time zone, and the best time to redeem a thirty- to sixty-minute, no-obligation transformation consultation in person, by phone, or via Zoom.

www.RowenaStarling.com
www.EmotionEmancipation.com
www.SaveYourBreath101.com

(510) 779-2486

BOOK ROWENA STARLING TO SPEAK AT YOUR NEXT EVENT

For your next event, you will find few professional speakers who will leave your audience or colleagues with more renewed passion for life than Rowena Starling. She is one of the most gifted speakers in the world. Since 1980, she has spoken to a wide variety of audiences and has received many standing ovations.

Whether your audience is ten or ten thousand and in North America or abroad, Rowena can deliver a customized message for your meeting or conference. She understands your audience does not want to be *taught* anything, but is interested in hearing stories of inspiration, joy, and achievement.

Rowena's speaking style is humorous and entertaining. It will inspire your audience to pursue their passions and aspire to achieving excellence in all their endeavors. If you're looking for a memorable speaker who will leave your audience wanting more, book Rowena today!

To find out whether Rowena is available to speak at your next meeting or event, visit her website or call.

www.RowenaStarling.com

(510) 779-2486

NOTES:

NOTES:

NOTES:

NOTES: